Nouveau
Cahier du jour
Cahier du soir

6e

11-12 ans

Anglais LV1

Auteurs

Nicole de Vannoise
Jean Cureau
Professeurs d'Anglais au collège

Auteur du mémento

Coline Segonne
Professeur d'Anglais au collège

MAGNARD

Présentation

Un cahier complet

- **Ce cahier d'Anglais, destiné aux élèves de 6e, est conforme aux derniers programmes.** Il reprend toutes les notions et couvre tous les domaines.
- **La rubrique « J'observe et je retiens »** propose toutes les **règles** accompagnées d'**exemples**, avec des **astuces** pour tout comprendre.
- **La rubrique « Je m'entraîne »** propose des **exercices progressifs** pour réinvestir les acquisitions. Ils sont classés par niveau de difficulté (de ★ à ★★★).
- À la fin de chaque page, l'enfant est invité à **s'auto-évaluer**.

→ Les corrigés détachables sont situés au centre du cahier.

Un mémento visuel

Un mémento avec l'essentiel à retenir en Anglais 6e : pour une mémorisation visuelle efficace !

→ À détacher au centre du cahier et à conserver toute l'année.

POUR LE CAHIER :
Illustration de couverture : Anne Guillard – **Illustrations intérieures :** Laurent Audoin
Conception graphique (couverture) : Yannick Le Bourg et Raphaël Hadid – **Mise en pages :** Facompo – **Cartographie :** Valérie Goncalves, Marie-Christine Liennard, Christel Parolini

POUR LE MÉMENTO VISUEL DÉTACHABLE :
Illustrations : Aurélie Verdon – **Mise en pages :** Linéale

Sommaire

VOCABULAIRE ET CIVILISATION

GRAMMAIRE

ANNEXES

Mémento visuel détachable

Corrigés détachables au centre du cahier

1 La maison
The house

→ Corrigés p. I

J'observe et je retiens

■ **Outside the house**

■ **Inside the house**

- **In the bedroom:** 1 bed 2 carpet 3 lamp 4 cupboard
- **In the bathroom:** 5 bathtub 6 washbasin 7 mirror 8 tap 9 washing machine
- **In the lounge:** 10 chair 11 TV set 12 table 13 armchair 14 sofa 15 picture 16 bookcase
- **In the kitchen:** 17 sink 18 cooker 19 dishwasher 20 fridge 21 freezer.

Je m'entraîne

1 ★ Regarde bien les dessins et les mots en bas de la page précédente, puis complète les phrases suivantes.

1. In the bedroom

a. I sleep in a ....

b. On the small table, there is a ....

c. On the floor, there is one ....

d. I put away clothes in a ....

2. In the bathroom

a. I have a bath in the ....

b. I wash my face and my hands in the ....

c. I look at myself in the ....

d. And I mustn't forget to turn off the ....

2 ★★ *In the kitchen*. À quoi servent les différents appareils et objets ménagers ? Lis bien les débuts de phrases et relie chacun à l'objet qui convient.

1. I wash vegetables... •	• a. in the freezer.
2. I cook dishes... •	• b. in the fridge.
3. I wash up dirty plates and glasses... •	• c. in the dishwasher.
4. I keep meat, vegetables, fruit juice... •	• d. in the sink.
5. I keep food for a long time... •	• e. in the cupboard.
6. I put away clean plates and glasses... •	• f. on and in the cooker.

3 ★★★ *In the lounge*. À quel meuble te fait penser chacune des phrases suivantes ?

1. I like reading. ....
2. What's on tonight? ....
3. The three of you, please sit on the... ....
4. I like to sit comfortably. ....
5. It's more comfortable than a... ....
6. Put the glasses and cups on the... ....
7. This painter is very good. ....

4 ★★★ *Outside the house*. Regarde bien le dessin en haut de la page précédente et réponds aux questions suivantes.

1. How many windows are there?

....

2. Where is the door?

....

3. How many chimneys can you see?

....

4. What is there on the left of the house?

....

5. What can you see in the sky?

....

6. What is there in the middle of the garden?

....

7. What colour are they?

....

8. What's in the garage?

....

5 ★★★ Pour chacune de ces phrases, choisis la bonne solution puis récris la phrase en entier. Regarde bien la page de gauche.

1. There is a (bath – bed – bookcase) in my bedroom.

....

2. I have a (washbasin – dishwasher – freezer) in my bathroom.

....

....

3. Look at my (armchair – carpet – fridge) in the kitchen.

....

4. My (TV set – car – bed) is in the garage.

....

Auto évaluation — Très bien ☐ Bien ☐ Pas assez bien ☐

2 La famille
The family

→ Corrigés p. I

J'observe et je retiens

■ Le féminin et le masculin

Male	Man	Boy	Son	Brother	Husband	Grandfather
Female	Woman	Girl	Daughter	Sister	Wife	Grandmother

■ L'âge

– Comment demander son âge à quelqu'un ? → *How old are you?*
– Comment donner son âge à quelqu'un ? → *I am (number) years old.*
C'est toujours le verbe ***be*** qui est utilisé.
– À la 3e personne du singulier, la question devient donc : → *How old is he/she?*
et la réponse : → *He/she is (number) years old.*

Je m'entraîne

1 ★ Relis les prénoms de la page précédente puis complète les phrases avec le bon prénom.

1. This is my sister .... ; she is a baby.
2. And that's my brother .... ; he is older than me.
3. My parents' names are .... and ....
4. I've got two grandfathers; they are very old! My mother's father's name is ....
5. My other grandfather is .... , of course. He smokes the pipe.
6. My father's mother's name is ....
7. My other grandmother's name is ....

2 ★★ En utilisant les informations de la page précédente, complète les phrases suivantes.

1. Robert is Susan's ....
2. Victoria is James's ....
3. William is James and Victoria's ....
4. Victoria is Patricia's ....
5. Jane is John's ....
6. .... , ... and .... are men.
7. .... , ... and .... are women.
8. .... , ... and .... are children.

3 ★★ Complète les phrases suivantes en te mettant à la place de Peter.

1. I call my .... Mum or Mummy.
2. I call my .... Dad or Daddy.
3. I call my .... Grandpa.
4. I call my .... Granny.
5. I call my .... Jack.
6. I call my .... Pat.

4 ★★★ À partir des indications suivantes, retrouve l'âge de chacun des membres de la famille de Peter et inscris-le dans le tableau.

1. I am eleven and my sister is one.
2. John is two years older than me.
3. My mother is thirty-four.
4. Her father is thirty years older.
5. My two grandfathers are the same age.
6. Susan is two years younger than her husband.
7. My other grandmother is five years younger than my mother's mother.
8. What about my father? Well, he is four years older than his wife.

Name	Age
Peter	
Patricia	
John	
Jane	
William	
Robert	
Susan	
James	
Victoria	

5 ★★★ En utilisant le vocabulaire de la page précédente, présente ta famille en quelques lignes.

....
....
....
....
....
....
....
....
....

Auto évaluation — Très bien ☐ Bien ☐ Pas assez bien ☐

3 Les repas
Meals

→ Corrigés p. I

J'observe et je retiens

Drinks

water · tea · wine · beer · soda · coffee · milk · orange juice · chocolate

Meat

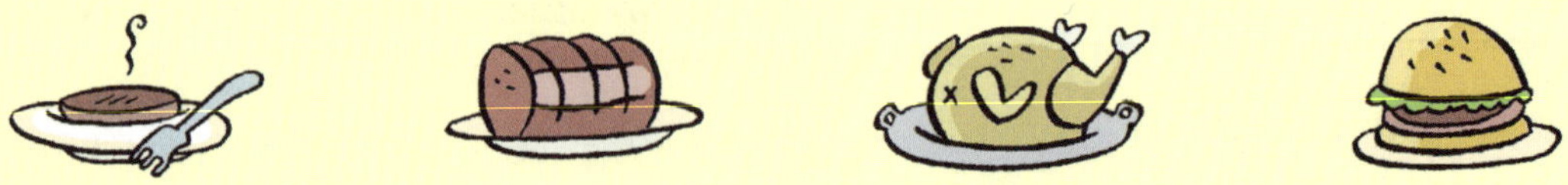

steak · roastbeef · chicken · hamburger

Vegetables

potatoes · carrots · peas · tomatoes · lettuce

Sweets

tart · pie · biscuits · cake · ice-cream

Fruit

orange · banana · apple · cherries

Don't forget!

bread · cereals · butter · toast · fish

Utensils

a glass · a cup · a bowl · a bottle · a fork · a knife · a spoon · a plate

Je m'entraîne

1 ★★ Tous les mots ont perdu leurs voyelles. Retrouve-les, puis place les mots complétés dans le tableau.

1. PTT ....
2. CHCKN ....
3. SPN ....
4. CHCLT ....
5. WTR ....
6. MLK ....
7. CFF ....
8. STK ....
9. P ....
10. PS ....
11. CRRT ....
12. PLT ....
13. RSTBF ....
14. KNF ....
15. C-CRM ....

Vegetables	Meat	Sweets	Drinks	Utensils

2 ★★ Pour manger et boire, on a besoin d'ustensiles. Complète les phrases suivantes avec le nom de l'ustensile approprié.

1. I eat soup out of a plate or out of a .... , with a ....
2. I eat meat with a .... and a ....
3. I drink tea out of a ....
4. In the morning, I drink coffee and milk out of a ....
5. I drink soda out of a glass or from the ....

3 ★★★ Écris tout ce que tu pourrais boire et manger au petit déjeuner.

Drinks: ...., ...,
............................, ...,
............................, ...

Food: ...., ...,
............................, ...,
............................, ...,
............................, ...,
............................, ...,
............................, ...

4 ★★★ Rédige les menus de deux personnes : l'une est au régime, l'autre est très gourmande.

Personne au régime

Lunch: .... ; Dinner: .... ;
.... ; .... ;
.... ; .... ;
....

Personne très gourmande

Lunch: .... ; Dinner: .... ;
.... ; .... ;
.... ; .... ;
....

Auto évaluation Très bien ☐ Bien ☐ Pas assez bien ☐

4 Le temps/Les nombres
Time/Numbers

→ Corrigés p. I

J'observe et je retiens

■ What's the time?

ten to twelve

twelve o'clock

ten past twelve

half past ten

a quarter past four

- Pour dire l'heure, on **commence par les minutes**.
- Si les minutes sont en deçà de l'heure, on utilise ***to***.

Exemple *It's ten to twelve.*

- Pour donner l'heure exacte, on utilise ***o'clock***.

Exemple *It's twelve o'clock.*

- Si les minutes sont au-delà de l'heure, on utilise ***past***.

Exemple *It's ten past twelve.*

- Pour la demi-heure, on utilise toujours ***half past***.

Exemple *It's half past ten.*

- Pour exprimer les quarts d'heure, on utilise ***a quarter past*** ou ***a quarter to***.

Exemple *It's a quarter past four.*

- Ce n'est que dans les horaires que l'on peut juxtaposer les heures et les minutes : *My train leaves at eleven fifty.*

Dans ce cas, on précise :

a.m.: le matin ou **p.m.**: l'après-midi ou le soir

Exemples *8 a.m.*: 8 heures du matin
2 p.m.: 2 heures de l'après-midi.

■ What's the day?

Sunday – Monday – Tuesday – Wednesday – Thursday – Friday – Saturday.

■ What's the month? What's the season?

Spring	Summer	Autumn	Winter
March	June	September	December
April	July	October	January
May	August	November	February

■ What's the date?

It's	*Tuesday*	*the*	*second*	*of*	*December,*	*two thousand*	*and*	*fourteen.*
	jour	***the***	nombre ordinal	***of***	mois	siècle	***and***	année.

■ Les nombres ordinaux

First, second, third…, twenty-second…, thirty-first…
Fourth, sixth, seventh…, tenth, eleventh…, thirteenth…

> **Attention**
> On écrit : *fifth* (5e), *eighth* (8e), *ninth* (9e), *twelfth* (12e).

> **Attention**
> À l'exception de *first, second, third* et de leurs composés, tous les nombres ordinaux se terminent par *-th*.

Je m'entraîne

1 ★★ Reporte les heures sur les montres « digitales » ci-dessous.

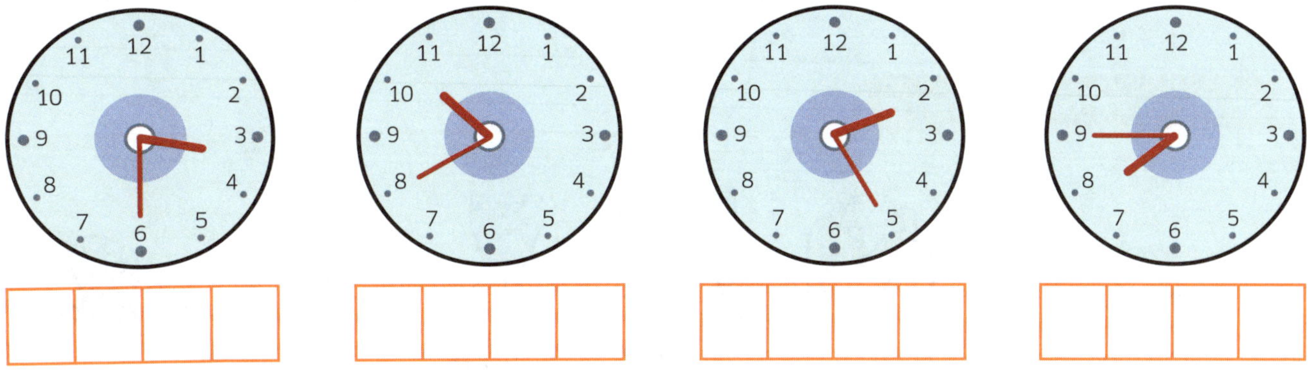

Écris chacune de ces heures en toutes lettres de la façon habituelle, puis comme un horaire.

1. .... ; ....
2. .... ; ....
3. .... ; ....
4. .... ; ....

2 ★★ Écris en chiffres les heures suivantes.

1. Nineteen to six: ....
2. A quarter to four: ....
3. Twenty-nine past four: ....
4. Two to two: ....

3 ★★★ Fais les opérations suivantes et écris les résultats en toutes lettres.

1. 414 + 141 = ...
2. 414 – 141 = ...

Rappel
En anglais, on met une **virgule** après mille et un **point** avant les décimales.

4 ★★★ Écris en toutes lettres les dates suivantes.

1. Samedi 10 septembre 1927

....

2. Lundi 2 décembre 1935

....

3. Mardi 12 mars 2018

....

4. Ta date de naissance (demande le jour de la semaine à tes parents)

....

5. Vendredi 5 juin 1992

....

6. Jeudi 15 septembre 1966

....

Auto évaluation Très bien ☐ Bien ☐ Pas assez bien ☐

5 Le corps/Les vêtements
The body/Clothes

→ Corrigés p. I

J'observe et je retiens

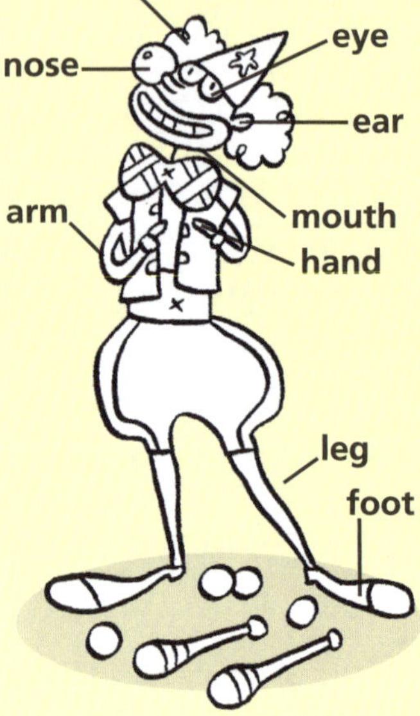

a coat

an overcoat

a dress

a (mini) skirt

sneakers

socks

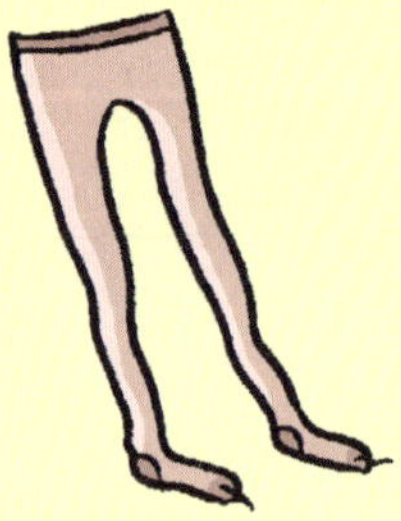
tights

a sweater

a pair of shoes

a pair of trainers

a cap

a hat

(a pair of) glasses

(a pair of) sunglasses

(a pair of) trousers

(a pair of) jeans

an umbrella

young

old

small and fat

tall and slim

strong

Je m'entraîne

1 ★ Colorie le clown de la page 12 en suivant les indications ci-dessous.

His face is pink (= red + white).
His hair is yellow.
His nose is red.
His mouth is red and there is white around it.
His trousers are black and red.
His big shoes are black.
His jacket is made of squares which are alternatively yellow and green.

2 ★ Relie les éléments de gauche aux noms de droite pour que les phrases aient un sens.

1. I can see with… •	• a. my legs and feet.
2. I can hear with… •	• b. my hand(s).
3. I can smell with… •	• c. my eyes.
4. I can speak and eat with… •	• d. my ears.
5. I can take things with… •	• e. my mouth.
6. I walk with… •	• f. my nose.

3 ★★ Voici des noms de vêtements qui se ressemblent en anglais et en français. Retrouve-les dans les mots dont les lettres ont été brouillées.

1. i h r s t T → T- ……………………
2. a e b l r z → b ……………………
3. a a o k n r → a ……………………
4. h o r s s t → s ……………………
5. a j n e s → j ……………………
6. s j a m y p a → p ……………………

4 ★★ Tous ces mots ont été coupés en trois morceaux ! À toi de les recoller. Barre les morceaux dès que tu les as utilisés. Ils ne peuvent servir qu'une fois. La première lettre de chaque mot est dans la première colonne.

C	RE	KS

1. ……………………………………

D	HO	NS

2. ……………………………………

J	RAI	SS

3. ……………………………………

S	OC	SERS

4. ……………………………………

T	OA	TER

5. ……………………………………

T	EA	SES

6. ……………………………………

G	WEA	RT

7. ……………………………………

S	KI	NERS

8. ……………………………………

S	ROU	T

9. ……………………………………

S	LAS	ES

10. ……………………………………

5 ★★★ Réponds aux questions suivantes.

1. In the morning, what do you put on?
……………………………………
2. What do you wear in winter?
……………………………………
3. When and where do you wear sunglasses?
……………………………………
4. When do you take an umbrella?
……………………………………
5. Do you wear socks in summer?
……………………………………
6. What does a golf player wear on his head?
……………………………………
……………………………………
7. What do you wear in summer?
……………………………………

Auto évaluation — Très bien ☐ Bien ☐ Pas assez bien ☐

6 Les activités
Activities

→ Corrigés p. I

J'observe et je retiens

■ Tous les personnages sont très actifs. Regarde leurs activités. Ce qu'ils font s'exprime à l'aide de verbes terminés par *-ing* et introduits par le verbe **be**.

- On exprime ainsi **ce que l'on voit au moment où on le voit**.
- On répond de cette manière à la question : *what is he/she doing?*
- Attention à l'orthographe des verbes en *-ing*.

Terminaison du verbe	Modification	Exemples
Consonne + « e »	le « e » disparaît	*having, phoning, making*
Verbe d'une seule syllabe terminé par 1 voyelle seule + 1 consonne	la consonne est doublée	*running, swimming*

Remarque
Pour tous les autres verbes, on ajoute *-ing* à la base verbale (ex. : *sleep* → *sleeping*).

He is having his breakfast.

She is washing her body.

He is cooking a dish.

He is doing the shopping.

She is hoovering the carpet.

She is making her bed.

He is drinking an orange juice.

She is eating an apple.

She is phoning her best friend.

He is sleeping in an armchair.

They are watching a DVD.

He is listening to a CD.

He is reading comics.

He is running to the stadium.

She is walking to school.

He is waiting at the traffic lights.

She is jumping over the gate.

He is playing football.

She is skiing in the mountain.

He is swimming in the swimming-pool.

Je m'entraîne

1 ★★ Pour chacune de ces images, tu as le choix entre deux solutions : une seule est correcte. Choisis la bonne et fais une phrase en prenant modèle sur celles de la page précédente.

1. go downstairs/fall downstairs

2. get up/go to bed

3. catch a ball/ kick a ball

4. wash up/ clean the kitchen

5. dance/fight

1. ....
2. ....
3. ....
4. ....
5. ....

2 ★★★ Ces trois amis sont bien différents. À partir des indications de caractère qui te sont données, construis des phrases décrivant ce qu'ils font en classe *(What are they doing?)*.

George is a very good student. Richard is not a very good student. Anthony is always day-dreaming.

Activités = – write what the teacher says
– not listen to the teacher
– read a book silently
– talk to his neighbour
– play with his pens
– think of his holidays
– laugh
– draw skeletons on paper
– learn his lesson
– listen to the birds outside
– think of his birthday party

1. George ....
George ....
George ....
2. Richard ....
Richard ....
Richard ....
Richard ....
3. Anthony ....
Anthony ....
Anthony ....
Anthony ....

3 ★★★ Qu'aimes-tu faire ? Que détestes-tu faire ? *(What do you like doing? What do you hate doing?)*

1. At school:

a. I like ....
....

b. I hate ....
....

2. At home:

a. I like ....
....

b. I hate ....
....

7 Réactions et sentiments
Reactions and feelings

→ Corrigés p. I

J'observe et je retiens

angry

bored

disappointed

happy

pleased

proud

ridiculous

sad

scared

serious

surprised

tired

laughing

smiling

She looks pretty, nice, beautiful! marvellous! fantastic!

He looks silly, stupid! horrible! awful!

The match was interesting, good, exciting! great! marvellous! fantastic!

Je m'entraîne

1 ★★ Voici une série d'adjectifs (dont beaucoup ressemblent aux mots français correspondants). Classe-les en trois catégories dans le tableau ci-dessous. Selon toi, quels sont ceux qui sont positifs, négatifs… ou ni l'un, ni l'autre ?

right – impossible – good – nice – beautiful – true – popular – sure – correct – different – easy – famous – silly – great – awful – horrible – wrong – interesting – delicious – lucky – bad – marvellous – fantastic – pretty – favourite – difficult – exciting – strange – stupid – clever – terrible – fine – dangerous.

Positive	Negative	Neither
....	....	....
....	....	....
....	....	....
....	....	....
....	....	....
....	....	....
....	....	....
....	....	....
....	....	....
....	....	....

2 ★★★ Découvre à quelles situations correspondent les sentiments ci-dessous. Écris les lettres dans le tableau ci-contre.

1. I get angry… — a. when other people smile.
2. I get bored… — b. when somebody laughs at me.
3. I'm disappointed… — c. when I've worked all day long.
4. I'm happy… — d. when I don't get a good mark.
5. I'm pleased… — e. when I do my homework.
6. I'm proud… — f. when I get the best mark.
7. I feel ridiculous… — g. when my best friend cries.
8. I'm sad… — h. when I have nothing to do.
9. I feel scared… — i. when I'm told a funny story.
10. I'm serious… — j. when I open my Christmas presents.
11. I'm surprised… — k. when I hear an extraordinary piece of news.
12. I feel tired… — l. when all my friends wish me a happy birthday.
13. I laugh… — m. when I am alone in the street at night.
14. I smile… — n. when I say something silly.

1.	2.	3.	4.	5.	6.	7.	8.	9.	10.	11.	12.	13.	14.

3 ★★★ Écris une phrase pour chaque adjectif proposé.

1. Awful → ....
2. Lucky → ....
3. Bored → ....
4. Proud → ....
5. Scared → ....
6. Sad → ....
7. Tired → ....
8. Happy → ....

Auto évaluation — Très bien ☐ Bien ☐ Pas assez bien ☐

8 Les îles Britanniques
The British Isles

→ Corrigés p. I

J'observe et je retiens

- Les îles Britanniques *(**the British Isles**)* se composent de deux grandes îles : la Grande-Bretagne *(**Great Britain**)* et l'Irlande *(**Ireland**)*.
- Le Royaume-Uni *(**the United Kingdom**)* comprend quatre régions : l'Angleterre *(**England**)*, l'Écosse *(**Scotland**)*, le pays de Galles *(**Wales**)* et l'Irlande du Nord *(**Northern Ireland**)*.
- La Grande-Bretagne est constituée de l'Écosse, de l'Angleterre et du pays de Galles.

À savoir
Le Tournoi des Six Nations, en rugby, voit s'affronter les trois équipes de Grande-Bretagne, l'Irlande, la France et l'Italie.

Je m'entraîne

1 ★ Pour finir la phrase, remets dans l'ordre les lettres du dernier mot et écris-le.

1. London is the capital of
A-D-E-G-L-N-N ....
2. Edinburgh is the capital of
A-C-D-L-N-O-S-T ....
3. Cardiff is the capital of
A-E-L-S-W ....
4. Belfast is the capital of
E-H-N-N-O-R-R-T-A-D-E-I-L-N-R ....

2 ★ L'un des symboles de la France est le coq. Réunis par une flèche les régions du Royaume-Uni et le symbole qui leur correspond.

1. England • • a. The leek
2. Northern Ireland • • b. The rose
3. Scotland • • c. The shamrock
4. Wales • • d. The thistle

3 ★★ Découvre les adjectifs correspondant aux noms des parties du Royaume-Uni dans ce mystérieux rectangle (ils sont tous à l'horizontale). Puis inscris-les en face des noms des régions.

1. England ....
2. Wales ....
3. Scotland ....
4. Northern Ireland ....
5. All these people are ....
(cet adjectif est écrit verticalement dans le rectangle.)

N	A	B	M	B	R	T	U	V
P	Q	E	I	R	I	S	H	W
K	O	G	T	I	S	H	E	J
Z	S	C	O	T	T	I	S	H
E	N	G	L	I	S	H	F	L
V	W	E	L	S	H	A	C	F
H	O	T	U	H	R	I	T	I

4 ★★ Regarde la carte et complète les phrases avec *bigger than* ou *smaller than*.

1. England is .... Scotland.
2. Scotland is .... Wales.
3. Wales is .... England.
4. Northern Ireland is .... Scotland.
5. Scotland is .... England.
6. Wales .... Northern Ireland.

5 ★★ En relisant l'exercice 4, que peux-tu en conclure ? Utilise un superlatif.

1. England is .... of all.
2. Northern Ireland is .... of all.

6 ★★ En t'aidant de la page précédente, complète les phrases suivantes.

1. The British Isles are made up of .... and ....
2. England, Scotland, ... and .... form the ....
3. Great Britain is made up of ...., ... and ....
4. The symbols of these regions are ...., ..., ... and ....

7 ★★★ Regarde bien la carte et la rose des vents page 18, puis complète les phrases suivantes.

Exemple Wales is **in the west of** England.

1. Scotland is .... England.
2. Ireland is .... England.
3. England is .... Scotland.
4. England is .... Wales.
5. Wales is .... Ireland.

Auto évaluation Très bien ☐ Bien ☐ Pas assez bien ☐

9 Visite de Londres
Visiting London

→ Corrigés p. II

J'observe et je retiens

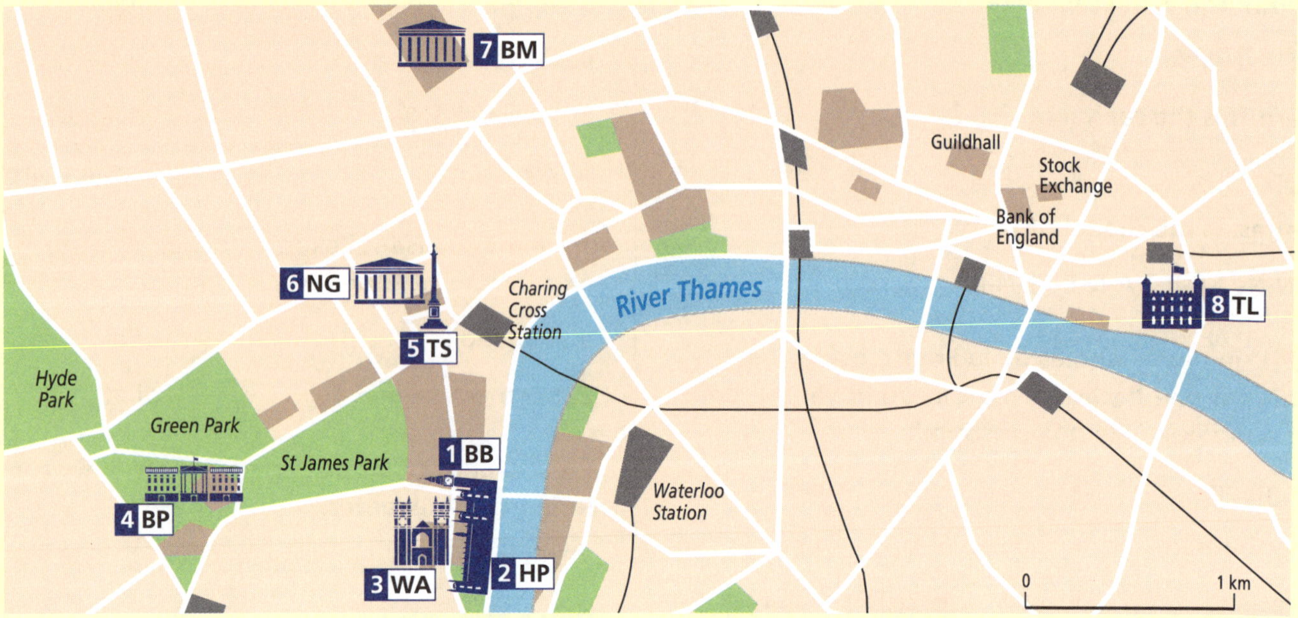

1

Big Ben

2

Houses of Parliament

3

Westminster Abbey

4

Buckingham Palace

1

clock

2

members

3
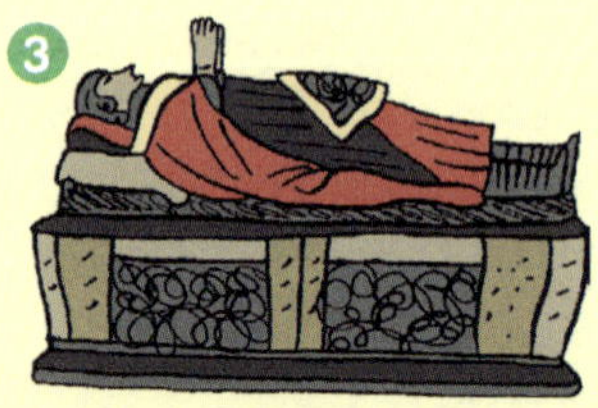
tombs

4

the Queen

5

Trafalgar Square

6

National Gallery

7

British Museum

8

the Tower of London

5

Nelson's column

6

a painting

7

mummies

8

jewels

Je m'entraîne

1 ★ Il y a tant de choses à voir à Londres ! En voici huit :

Big Ben	the British Museum	Buckingham Palace	the Houses of Parliament
the National Gallery	the Tower of London	Trafalgar Square	Westminster Abbey

Souligne toutes les lettres en capitales. Puis réunis-les 2 par 2 ; **ex. :** pour Big Ben : B.B.

....

2 ★★ Maintenant, regarde le plan de la page 20. Tu y vois de petits rectangles qui comportent un numéro et deux lettres en capitales. C'est là que se trouve chaque monument. Dans le tableau ci-dessous, écris le nom du monument et le chiffre qui lui correspond.

	Monument	N°		Monument	N°
B.B.	Big Ben		**B.M.**		
B.P.			**H.P.**		
N.G.			**T.L.**		
T.S.			**W.A.**		

3 ★★★ Complète les phrases suivantes qui répondent à la question "What/Who can you see" …?

1. … in Buckingham Palace?

....

2. … in the Houses of Parliament?

....

3. … in Trafalgar Square?

....

4. … near Westminster Abbey?

....

4 ★★★ Complète les phrases suivantes qui répondent à la question "Where can you find"…?

1. … paintings ?

....

2. … the jewels of the crown ?

....

3. … tombs?

....

4. … mummies?

....

Help

Abbey: abbaye
Clock: horloge
Column: colonne
Jewels: joyaux
Mummy: momie
Near: près
Paintings: tableaux
Palace: palais
Queen: reine
Tomb: tombe
M.P.s (members of the Parliament): membres du Parlement

5 ★★★ Recherche qui était Nelson, puis écris-le ci-dessous, en français.

....

....

....

....

....

....

....

....

Auto évaluation Très bien ☐ Bien ☐ Pas assez bien ☐

10 Les animaux dans le Commonwealth
Animals in the Commonwealth

→ Corrigés p. II

J'observe et je retiens

Le Commonwealth est une association de 54 pays. La plupart étaient autrefois des colonies britanniques. On y parle toujours anglais. Bien que la reine soit à la tête du Commonwealth, les pays sont indépendants.

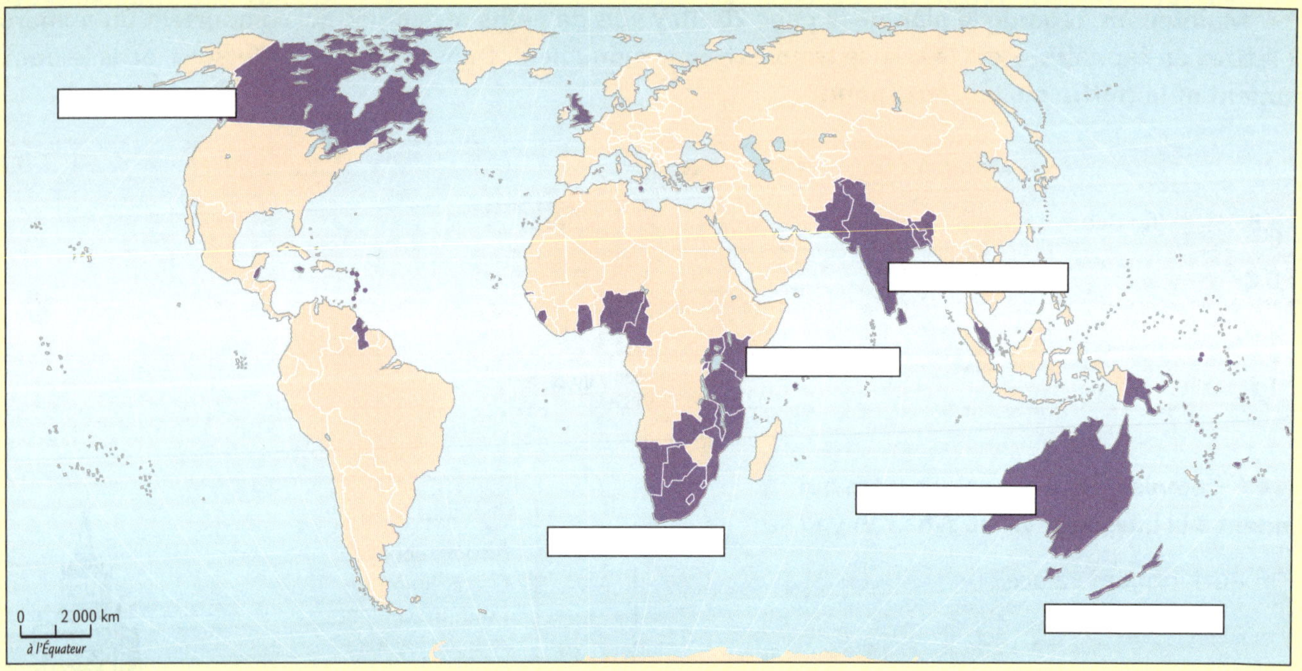

AUSTRALIA				
	....	....	....	....
CANADA				
	....	....	....	....
INDIA				
	....	....	....	....
KENYA				
	....	....	....	....
NEW ZEALAND				
	....	....	....	....
SOUTH AFRICA				
	....	....	....	....

Je m'entraîne

1 ★★ Sur la carte du monde de la page 22, six pays sont en violet. Recherche-les sur un atlas, dans un dictionnaire, sur Internet... Voici leurs noms en anglais, mais les lettres sont mélangées ; à toi de les remettre en ordre.

1. Aaailrstu → ....
2. aaaCdn → ....
3. adlin → ....
4. aeKny → ....
5. eNw aadelnZ → ....
6. hoStu Aacfir → ....

Reporte ces noms dans les rectangles sur la carte du monde.

2 ★★ Voici la liste des animaux représentés sur l'autre page : *caribou – dingo – elephant – elk – emu – giraffe – hippopotamus – kangaroo – kiwi – koala – lion – monkey – octopus – ostrich – panther – polar bear – rhinoceros – sheep – snake – springbok – tiger – whale – wolf – zebra.*

Remarque
Certains s'écrivent comme en français, d'autres ont une orthographe proche du français.

Écris leurs noms sous les images qui leur correspondent.

Pour ceux que tu ne connais pas, regarde en bas de la page (*Help*) et reporte leurs noms sous les images.

3 ★★★ En t'aidant des images de la page de gauche, relie les animaux aux pays où ils vivent.

1. kiwi •	
2. springbok •	
3. dingo •	• a. India
4. octopus •	• b. Canada
5. panther •	• c. Kenya
6. tiger •	• d. South Africa
7. polar bear •	• e. New Zealand
8. elephant •	• f. Australia
9. zebra •	
10. wolf •	

4 ★★★ Trouve les animaux qui correspondent à ces définitions :

1. A .... is a long reptile with no legs.
2. A .... lives in trees and eat leaves.
3. A .... has a very long neck and long legs.
4. A .... runs very fast and carries its babies in a pocket.
5. A .... is a very big animal which lives in the sea.
6. A .... has black and white lines on its body.
7. A .... looks like a big dog.
8. A .... is white and lives near the North Pole.
9. An .... lives in the sea and has eight tentacles.
10. A .... is a very big cat which lives in Asia.

Help
Dingo: sorte de chien sauvage
Elk: élan
Emu: émeu
Monkey: singe
Octopus: pieuvre
Polar bear: ours polaire
Snake: serpent
Whale: baleine
Wolf: loup

Auto évaluation Très bien ☐ Bien ☐ Pas assez bien ☐

11 Be

→ Corrigés p. II

J'observe et je retiens

– I'm John Smith. (1)
– I'm thirty. (2)
– I'm all right. (3)
– I'm from London. (4)
– I'm a mechanic. (5)
– My car's blue. (6)
– How much is it? (7)
– It's £ 6,000. (8)
– I'm happy. (9)
– Goodbye. I'm tired. (10)

Remarque
Ces phrases donnent des informations sur John Smith.

Conjugaison

- Affirmation :

	1re pers.	2e pers.	3e pers.
singulier	am	are	is
pluriel	are	are	are

- Négation : ***'m not; isn't; aren't***
- Interrogation : ***Are you?; Is he/she/it?***

Emploi

On peut employer ***be*** pour la **dénomination** (phrase 1) ; l'**âge** (phrase 2) ; la **santé** (phrase 3) ; l'**origine** (phrase 4) ; le **métier** (phrase 5) ; la **couleur** (phrase 6) ; le **prix** (phrases 7 et 8) ; les **sentiments** (phrase 9) ; les **sensations** (phrase 10).

Mais aussi pour l'**heure** : *It's two o'clock.*

Je m'entraîne

1 ★ Transforme les phrases suivantes en phrases négatives ou interrogatives selon les indications.

1. Andrew is from Cambridge. *(négative)*

....

2. He is a mechanic. *(interrogative)*

....

3. He is very old. *(négative)*

....

4. His parents are in Cambridge. *(interrogative)*

....

2 ★★ Lis les informations suivantes et relie les questions aux réponses correspondantes.

Mary is twenty-two. She lives in London. She likes mathematics. She's got a blue car. Today the weather is fine. She is happy. She has friends in Paris.

1. Is Mary very old? •
2. Is she good at mathematics? •
3. Are her friends in London? •
4. Is her car blue? •
5. Is it raining today? •

• a. Yes, she is.
• b. No, they aren't.
• c. No, it isn't.
• d. Yes, it is.
• e. No, she isn't.

3 ★★ Réponds aux questions suivantes concernant John Smith (relis la rubrique « J'observe et je retiens »).

1. Where is he from? ....
2. What is he? ....
3. What colour is his car? ....
4. How old is he? ....
5. How is he? ....
6. Is his car expensive or cheap? ....

Auto évaluation Très bien ☐ Bien ☐ Pas assez bien ☐

12 Have

→ Corrigés p. II

J'observe et je retiens

– I've got a sister. She's got a nice cat. Her cat has got a long tail. (1)
– At seven o'clock a.m., I have my breakfast. But yesterday I had it at nine. (2)
– Have a nice lunch! Have a pleasant journey! (3)

Conjugaison

- Présent :

	1re pers.	2e pers.	3e pers.
singulier	**have**	**have**	**has**
pluriel	**have**	**have**	**have**

- Passé :

	1re pers.	2e pers.	3e pers.
singulier	**had**	**had**	**had**
pluriel	**had**	**had**	**had**

Emploi

- Phrase 1 : en langage familier, ***have got*** exprime généralement la **possession** ;
  – négation : *haven't got, hasn't got*;
  – interrogation : *have you got…? has she got…?*
- Phrase 2 : ***have*** est un **verbe ordinaire** ;
  – négation : *I don't have, he doesn't have*;
  – interrogation : *do you have…? does she have…?*
- Phrase 3 : dans les **expressions de souhait**, ***have*** ne se traduit pas.

Je m'entraîne

1 ★ Écris ce que chacun possède.
Utilise les mots : *camera*, *house*, *bike*.

1. Me 2. My sister 3. My parents

1. ....
....
....

2. ....
....
....

3. ....
....
....

2 ★★ Réponds aux questions suivantes positivement et négativement.

1. Have you got any brothers or sisters?

⊕ .... ⊖ ....

2. Has your father got a motorbike?

⊕ .... ⊖ ....

3 ★★★ Réponds aux questions suivantes en utilisant les éléments indiqués entre parenthèses.

1. At what time do English people have tea? (5 p.m.)

....
....
....

2. Where do you have a nice lunch? (at a restaurant)

....
....
....

Auto évaluation Très bien ☐ Bien ☐ Pas assez bien ☐

13 *There is/there are, how many?*

→ Corrigés p. II

J'observe et je retiens

Mr Write – **How many rooms are there downstairs?**

Mr Black – **There are** three rooms.

Mr Write – **Is there** a garage near your house?

Mr Black – Yes, **there is**.

Construction

- *There **is*** + nom **singulier**
- *There **are*** + nom **pluriel**

Emploi

- *There is/are* sert à **décrire**.

Exemple *There is a TV set in the lounge.*

- On le trouve aussi en réponse à la question *How many?* pour indiquer **une quantité**.

Exemple *There are three rooms.*

Je m'entraîne

1 ★ Regarde bien l'image et réponds aux questions.

1. How many windows are there?

....

2. How many doors are there?

....

3. How many children are there on the roof?

....

4. Are there two chimneys?

....

5. Is there a car in front of the house?

....

2 ★★ Complète ce dialogue en utilisant *there is/there are* (formes affirmative, négative ou interrogative) selon le sens de la phrase.

1. "Where can I park my car?
– .... a parking on Madison Street."

2. " .... a bank on this street?"
– No, ... but .... one on Bloomsbury Avenue."

3. "I'm hungry. Where .... a restaurant?
– .... a lot of restaurants, but .... a very good one near the station."

3 ★★★ Décris cette image en utilisant *there is/there are* et les mots proposés. N'oublie pas d'indiquer le nombre d'objets.

1. (chairs) ....
2. (tables) ....
3. (board) ....
4. (bag) ....

Auto évaluation Très bien ☐ Bien ☐ Pas assez bien ☐

14 La phrase simple

→ Corrigés p. II

J'observe et je retiens

SUSAN – Is breakfast ready?
MUMMY – Yes, it's seven o'clock.
SUSAN – Can I have a cup of chocolate?
MUMMY – Of course, you can have one.
Hurry up! School begins at 8.
SUSAN – No, Mummy, it doesn't begin at 8 today.
MUMMY – Does it begin at 9 then?
SUSAN – Yes, it does.

Si le verbe est :	Forme négative	Forme interrogative
auxiliaire ou modal	sujet + **aux./modal** + *not*	**aux./modal** + sujet
ordinaire	sujet + ***do/does* + *not*** + base verbale	***do/does*** + sujet + base verbale

Rappel
Does s'emploie à la 3e personne du singulier du présent de l'indicatif.

Je m'entraîne

1 ★ Entoure le mot qui convient pour compléter les phrases.

1. Children generally .... like carrots. a. do b. don't c. can
2. .... they like soda? a. Does b. Do c. Is
3. .... your mother give you chips? a. Do b. Has got c. Does
4. Yes, but she .... give us beer. a. must b. does c. doesn't

2 ★★ Mets les phrases à la forme indiquée.

1. My sister eats soup with a fork. *(négative)*

....

2. My father drinks beer out of the bottle. *(interrogative)*

....

....

3. We often eat fish. *(négative)*

....

4. Fish is very expensive. *(interrogative)*

....

3 ★★★ Remets les mots dans l'ordre pour faire des phrases.

1. wine / do / drink / Children / not /.

....

....

2. end / is / good / lunch / at / the / Cheese / very / of / a /.

....

....

3. tea / a / Do / bowl / drink / out of / you / ?

....

....

Auto évaluation Très bien ☐ Bien ☐ Pas assez bien ☐

15 Le présent simple

→ Corrigés p. II

J'observe et je retiens

– I eatØ cereals every morning. (1)
– John eats cereals every morning too. (2)

– They watchØ television every night. (3)
– She watches television every night. (4)

- Un verbe au **présent simple** sert à indiquer une **habitude** (souvent soulignée par une marque de fréquence : *every*, *on*…).
- À la 3e pers. du singulier, le verbe se termine par *-s* (phrase 2) et par *-es* pour *do* et *go*.
- Lorsque le verbe se termine par *-s*, *-ch*, *-sh*, on ajoute *-es* au lieu de *-s* (phrase 4).
- Aux autres personnes, on n'ajoute rien (phrases 1 et 3).
- On indique qu'il n'y a rien à l'aide du signe Ø.

Exemple *I eatØ*.

Je m'entraîne

1 ★ Mets les verbes suivants au présent simple : ajoute *-s* ou *-es* quand c'est nécessaire ou le signe Ø quand il n'y a rien à ajouter.

1. He answer .... 2. We ask ....
3. The lesson begin ....
4. The wind blow .... 5. She break ....
6. They bring .... 7. Mary go ....
8. She dress .... 9. You buy ....
10. He wash .... 11. I like ....
12. She walk ....

2 ★★ Complète les phrases suivantes avec le verbe indiqué entre parenthèses à la forme du présent simple qui convient.

1. My parents .... me to get good marks. *(want)*
2. It is easy because I .... everything. *(remember)*
3. My sister .... everything. *(forget)*
4. She .... that it is too difficult to learn. *(say)*
5. My mother .... that she is lazy. *(think)*
6. When it is cold, Mary .... her coat. *(put on)*
7. When school is over, we always .... home. *(run)*
8. She .... to school by bus. *(go)*
9. Every Saturday, they .... tennis. *(play)*
10. My brother .... sports. *(love)*

3 ★★★ Relie les morceaux de phrases afin de former des phrases qui aient un sens.

1. Mary •	• like •	• football matches on Saturdays.
2. John •	• drinks •	• rugby every Monday.
3. My parents •	• eats •	• his bottles every morning.
4. My cat •	• play •	• classical music.
5. The milkman •	• watches •	• its milk before dinner.
6. They •	• brings •	• her breakfast at 7 o'clock.

Auto évaluation Très bien ☐ Bien ☐ Pas assez bien ☐

16 Le présent en *-ing*

→ Corrigés p. II

J'observe et je retiens

What's Tom doing? He is playing football.

Formation : ***be*** + base verbale + ***-ing***

Emploi

- Décrire ce que l'on voit, ce que l'on entend, ce que l'on ressent dans l'instant, **au moment où l'on parle**.

Exemple *She is eating an apple.*

- Dire ce qu'on a décidé de faire.

Exemple *I'm meeting him on Saturday.*

- Dire ce qui va sûrement se produire.

Exemple *The train is leaving at 4.*

Remarque
Le présent en *-ing* se traduit par un présent français.

Je m'entraîne

1 ★★ Que dirais-tu pour demander :

1. ce que fait Jennifer ? ....
2. où va Alison ? ....
3. si Rick joue au football ? ....
....
4. ce que font Rick et Paul ? ....
....

2 ★★ Fais des phrases avec les mots suivants en utilisant le présent en *-ing*.

1. I / leave / tomorrow /. ....
2. The / plane / land / at five /. ....
....
3. My father / meet / his boss / next / week /. ....
....

3 ★★★ Voici, dans l'ordre, les verbes à utiliser dans la description de l'image en haut de la page : *sleep* – *play* – *read* – *run* – *sail* – *swim* – *windsurf*. Écris ce que chaque personnage fait.

1. Liz ....
....
2. Rick and Paul ....
....
3. Jennifer ....
4. Peter ....
5. Alison ....
....
6. Bob ....
7. John ....
....

Auto évaluation Très bien ☐ Bien ☐ Pas assez bien ☐

17 Le passé

→ Corrigés p. II

J'observe et je retiens

Yesterday I **worked** hard at school. Then I **played** tennis. Later on I **went** shopping and **bought** a video. But I **didn't buy** any CDs. When I **came back** home my mother **asked** me: "What **did** you **buy**?"

Formation du passé

- Auxiliaires : *be* → *was/were* ; *have* → *had*
- Verbes réguliers : base verbale + *-ed*
- Forme négative : sujet + *did* + *not* + base verbale
- Forme interrogative : *did* + sujet + base verbale

Rappel
was → *wasn't* ; *were* → *weren't*

Je m'entraîne

1 ★★ Écris le passé (*simple past*) des verbes suivants.

1. play ....
2. spend ....
3. read ....
4. have ....
5. learn ....
6. see ....
7. catch ....
8. be ....
9. watch ....

2 ★★ Complète les phrases suivantes avec le passé de sept des verbes de l'exercice 1.

1. Last year I .... my holidays at the seaside.
2. I often .... on the beach.
3. When I was tired I .... a book.
4. I .... a lot of interesting things.
5. One day I .... a man with a heavy case.
6. What beautiful holidays I .... !
7. Last morning, I .... the bus.

Conseil
Tu peux t'aider de la liste des verbes irréguliers, page 56.

1 2 3 4 5

3 ★★★ Raconte ce qui s'est passé en utilisant les verbes suivants dans l'ordre indiqué : *go* – *take out* – *shout* – *run away* – *catch*.

1. ....
2. ....
3. ....
4. ....
5. ....

Auto évaluation Très bien ☐ Bien ☐ Pas assez bien ☐

Corrigés

VOCABULAIRE ET CIVILISATION

1 La maison — p. 5

1 1. a. bed – b. lamp – c. carpet – d. cupboard.
2. a. bathtub – b. washbasin – c. mirror – d. tap.

2 1. d. – 2. f. – 3. c. – 4. b. – 5. a. – 6. e.

3 1. bookcase – 2. TV set – 3. sofa – 4. armchair – 5. chair – 6. table – 7. picture.

4 1. There are seven windows. – 2. It is in the middle of the house/between two windows. – 3. I can see one (chimney). – 4. There is a garage (on the left of the house). – 5. I can see clouds in the sky. – 6. There are flowers in the middle of the garden. – 7. They are yellow. – 8. There is a car in the garage.

5 1. bed – 2. washbasin – 3. fridge – 4. car.

2 La famille — p. 7

1 1. Patricia – 2. John – 3. William and Jane – 4. Robert – 5. James – 6. Victoria – 7. Susan.

2 1. husband – 2. wife – 3. son – 4. grandmother – 5. mother – 6. Robert, James, William – 7. Susan, Victoria, Jane – 8. John, Peter, Patricia.

3 1. mother – 2. father – 3. grandfather – 4. grandmother – 5. brother – 6. sister.

4 Peter, 11 – Patricia, 1 – John, 13 – Jane, 34 – William, 38 – Robert, 64 – Susan, 62 – James, 64 – Victoria, 57.

5 À corriger avec un adulte.

3 Les repas — p. 9

1 1. potato – 2. chicken – 3. spoon – 4. chocolate – 5. water – 6. milk – 7. coffee – 8. steak – 9. pie – 10. peas – 11. carrot 12. plate – 13. roastbeef – 14. knife – 15. ice-cream.

Vegetables: potato, peas, carrot. – **Meat:** chicken, steak, roastbeef. – **Sweets:** pie, ice-cream. – **Drinks:** water, milk, coffee, chocolate. – **Utensils:** spoon, plate, knife.

2 1. bowl/spoon – 2. fork/knife – 3. cup – 4. bowl – 5. bottle.

3 **Drinks:** orange juice – tea – coffee – chocolate – milk – water. **Food:** bread – butter – toast – biscuits – cereals – cake – apples.

4 *Corrigé suggéré :*

Personne au régime : Lunch: tomatoes, carrots, chicken, an apple. **Dinner:** fish, lettuce, orange. **Personne très gourmande : Lunch:** roastbeef, chips, tart. **Dinner:** soup, hamburger, peas, potatoes, pie.

4 Le temps/Les nombres — p. 11

1 03.30 – 10.40 – 02.25 – 07.45.
1. half past three/three thirty. – 2. twenty to eleven/ten forty. 3. twenty-five past two/two twenty-five. – 4. a quarter to eight/seven forty-five.

2 1. 5 h 41 – 2. 3 h 45 – 3. 4 h 29 – 4. 1 h 58.

3 1. 555: five hundred and fifty-five. – 2. 273: two hundred and seventy-three.

4 1. Saturday, the tenth of September, nineteen hundred and twenty-seven. – 2. Monday, the second of December, nineteen hundred and thirty-five. – 3. Tuesday, the twelfth of March, two thousand and eighteen. – 4. À corriger avec un adulte. 5. Friday, the fifth of June, nineteen hundred and ninety-two. – 6. Thursday, the fifteenth of September, nineteen hundred and sixty-six.

5 Le corps/Les vêtements — p. 13

1 À corriger avec un adulte.

2 1. c. – 2. d. – 3. f. – 4. e. – 5. b. – 6. a.

3 1. T-shirt – 2. blazer – 3. anorak – 4. shorts – 5. jeans – 6. pyjamas.

4 1. coat – 2. dress – 3. jeans – 4. shoes – 5. trainers – 6. trousers – 7. glasses – 8. sweater – 9. skirt – 10. socks.

5 *Corrigé suggéré :* 1. In the morning, I put on socks, a T-shirt and jeans... and shoes. – 2. In winter I wear a sweater, an overcoat or an anorak or a blazer, and trousers of course! – 3. I wear sunglasses in winter in the mountains and in summer at the seaside. – 4. I take an umbrella when it rains. – 5. No, I don't. – 6. a cap. – 7. I wear a hat and sunglasses.

6 Les activités — p. 15

1 1. He is falling downstairs. – 2. She's getting up. – 3. He is kicking a ball. – 4. He's washing up. – 5. They are dancing.

2 *Corrigé suggéré :* 1. George is writing what the teacher says. George is reading a book silently. George is learning his lesson. – 2. Richard is not listening to the teacher. Richard is talking to his neighbour. Richard is playing with his pens. Richard is laughing. – 3. Anthony is thinking of his holidays. – Anthony is listening to the birds outside. – Anthony is drawing skeletons on paper. – Anthony is thinking of his birthday party.

3 *Corrigé suggéré :* 1. a. I like learning English. b. I hate answering questions. – 2. a. I like watching television. b. I hate making my bed.

7 Réactions et sentiments — p. 17

1 **Positive:** beautiful – clever – correct – delicious – easy – exciting – famous – fantastic – favourite – fine – good – great – interesting – lucky – marvellous – nice – popular – pretty – right – sure – true.
Negative: awful – bad – dangerous – difficult – horrible – impossible – silly – stupid – terrible – wrong.
Neither: different – strange.

2 1. b. – 2. h. – 3. d. – 4. l. – 5. j. – 6. f. – 7. n. – 8. g. – 9. m. – 10. e. – 11. k. – 12. c. – 13. i. – 14. a.

3 *Corrigé suggéré :* 1. I wanted to take a walk. Bad luck! The weather was awful. – 2. The bus was full up but I was lucky to find a seat. – 3. The TV programme was so uninteresting that I quickly got bored. – 4. Manchester won. All the players were very proud of their success. – 5. When I heard somebody walk in the house I felt scared to death. – 6. Peter has got a bad mark, he is sad. – 7. She didn't sleep well, she is very tired! – 8. I'm so happy because I received a good news.

8 Les îles Britanniques — p. 19

1 1. England – 2. Scotland – 3. Wales – 4. Northern Ireland.

2 1. b. – 2. c. – 3. d. – 4. a.

3 1. English – 2. Welsh – 3. Scottish – 4. Irish – 5. British.

4 1. bigger than – 2. bigger than – 3. smaller than – 4. smaller than – 5. smaller than. – 6. Wales is bigger than Northern Ireland.

5 1. England is the biggest of all. – 2. Northern Ireland is the smallest of all.

6 1. Great Britain ; Ireland. – 2. Wales ; Northern Ireland ; United Kingdom. – 3. Scotland ; England ; Wales. – 4. The thistle ; the rose ; the leek ; the shamrock.

Corrigés détachables

7 1. in the north of – 2. in the west of – 3. in the south of – 4. in the east of – 5. in the east of.

9 Visite de Londres p. 21

1 BB – BM – BP – HP – NG – TL – TS – WA.

2 Big Ben: 1 – Buckingham Palace: 4 – National Gallery: 6 – Trafalgar Square: 5 – British Museum: 7 – Houses of Parliament: 2 – Tower of London: 8 – Westminster Abbey: 3.

3 1. I can see the Queen in Buckingham Palace – 2. I can see members of Parliament in the Houses of Parliament – 3. I can see the statue of Nelson in Trafalgar Square – 4. I can see Big Ben near Westminster Abbey.

4 1. I can find paintings in the National Gallery. – 2. I can find the jewels of the crown in the Tower of London. – 3. I can find tombs in Westminster Abbey. – 4. I can find mummies in the British Museum.

5 Nelson fut l'amiral le plus célèbre de la flotte anglaise. Il est né en 1758 et il est mort à la bataille de Trafalgar en 1805.

10 Les animaux dans le Commonwealth p. 23

1 1. Australia – 2. Canada – 3. India – 4. Kenya – 5. New Zealand – 6. South Africa.

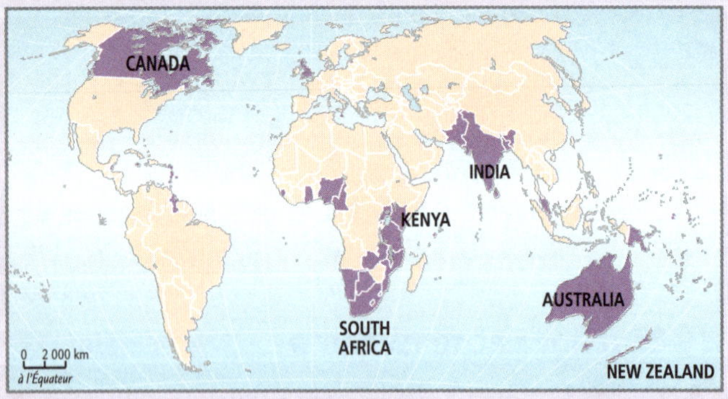

2 **Australia:** kangaroo; koala; emu; dingo – **Canada:** polar bear; wolf; caribou; elk – **India:** tiger; elephant; panther; snake – **Kenya:** giraffe; zebra; hippopotamus; ostrich – **New Zealand:** sheep; kiwi; octopus; whale – **South Africa:** springbok; rhinoceros; lion; monkey.

3 1. e. – 2. d. – 3. f. – 4. e. – 5. a. – 6. a. – 7. b. – 8. a. – 9. c. – 10. b.

4 1. snake – 2. koala – 3. giraffe – 4. kangaroo – 5. whale – 6. zebra – 7. wolf – 8. polar bear – 9. octopus – 10. tiger.

GRAMMAIRE

11 *Be* p. 24

1 1. Andrew isn't from Cambridge. – 2. Is he a mechanic? – 3. He isn't very old. – 4. Are his parents in Cambridge?

2 1. e. – 2. a. – 3. b. – 4. d. – 5. c.

3 1. He's from London. – 2. He's a mechanic. – 3. His car's blue. – 4. He's thirty. – 5. He's all right. – 6. It's cheap.

12 *Have* p. 25

1 1. I've got a bike. – 2. My sister's got a camera. – 3. My parents have got a house.

2 1. + Yes, I have/– No I haven't. – 2. + Yes, he has/– No he hasn't.

3 1. They have tea at 5 p.m. – 2. I have a nice lunch at a restaurant.

13 *There is/there are, how many?* p. 26

1 1. There are eight (windows). – 2. There is one (door). – 3. There are two (children on the roof). – 4. No, there aren't, there is one (chimney). – 5. No, there isn't.

2 1. There is. – 2. Is there/there isn't/there is. – 3. Is there/there are/there is.

3 1. There are nine chairs. – 2. There are four tables. – 3. There is one board. – 4. There is one bag.

14 La phrase simple p. 27

1 1. b. – 2. b. – 3. c. – 4. c.

2 1. My sister doesn't eat soup with a fork. – 2. Does your father drink beer out of the bottle? – 3. We don't often eat fish. – 4. Is fish very expensive?

3 1. Children do not drink wine. – 2. Cheese is very good at the end of a lunch. – 3. Do you drink tea out of a bowl?

15 Le présent simple p. 28

1 1. answers – 2. askØ – 3. begins – 4. blows – 5. breaks – 6. bringØ – 7. goes – 8. dresses – 9. buyØ – 10. washes – 11. likeØ – 12. walks.

2 1. want – 2. remember – 3. forgets – 4. says – 5. thinks – 6. puts on – 7. run – 8. goes – 9. play – 10. loves.

3 1. Mary eats her breakfast at 7 o'clock. – 2. John watches football matches on Saturdays. – 3. My parents like classical music. – 4. My cat drinks its milk before dinner. – 5. The milkman brings his bottles every morning. – 6. They play rugby every Monday.

16 Le présent en *-ing* p. 29

1 1. What's Jennifer doing? – 2. Where's Alison going? – 3. Is Rick playing football? – 4. What are Rick and Paul doing?

2 1. I'm leaving tomorrow. – 2. The plane is landing at five. 3. My father is meeting his boss next week.

3 1. Liz is sleeping on the beach. – 2. Rick and Paul are playing volley-ball. – 3. Jennifer is reading a book. – 4. Peter is running. 5. Alison is sailing. – 6. Bob is swimming. – 7. John is windsurfing.

17 Le passé p. 30

1 1. played – 2. spent – 3. read – 4. had – 5. learned – 6. saw – 7. caught – 8. was/were – 9. watched.

2 1. spent – 2. played – 3. read – 4. learned – 5. saw – 6. had – 7. caught.

3 *Corrigé suggéré :* 1. A gangster went into a bank. – 2. He took out his pistol. – 3. The clerk shouted. – 4. The gangster ran away. – 5. A policeman caught him.

18 *Can/can't* p. 31

1 1. a. The doctor can't come before twelve. b. Can the doctor come before twelve?
2. a. My friend Bob can't play the synthetizer. b. Can my friend Bob play the synthetizer?
3. a. My brother can't go to school alone. b. Can my brother go to school alone?
4. a. Emma can't drink milk. b. Can Emma drink milk?

2 1. I can swim. – 2. I can't swim two kilometres. – 3. I can't drive a car. – 4. I can't eat candy. – 5. I can read english. – 6. I can't draw.

3 *Corrigé suggéré :*
1. He/she can walk; he/she can make a puzzle. – 2. He/she can play in the garden; he/she can watch Disney videos. – 3. He/she can't cross over the street; he/she can't watch television after 8 p.m.

Mémento visuel
Anglais 6^e^

À détacher et à conserver toute l'année !

Conjuguer en anglais

Au présent

Le présent simple

- État, vérité générale ou habitude.
- *s* à la 3e personne du singulier

I like school.
She likes school.

- Forme négative :

I don't like school.
She doesn't like school.

- Forme interrogative :

Do you like school?
Does she like school?

Le présent en *be* + *-ing*

- Ce qui se passe au moment où l'on parle.
- Sujet + *be* conjugué au présent + BV-*ing*

I am watching TV.

- Forme négative :

I am not watching TV.

- Forme interrogative :

Are you watching TV?

Au passé

Le prétérit simple

- Action passée, datée, terminée, ponctuelle.
- Sujet + BV-*ed* ou verbe irrégulier.

I turned on the TV at 8 o'clock.
She ate an ice cream.

- Forme négative :

I did not turn on the TV at 8 o'clock.
She didn't eat an ice cream.

- Forme interrogative :

Did you turn on the TV at 8 o'clock?
Did she eat an ice cream?

Le prétérit en *be* + *-ing*

- Action en cours de déroulement dans le passé.

I was watching TV last night.

- Forme négative :

I was not watching TV last night.

- Forme interrogative :

Were you watching TV last night?

Les pronoms personnels

Les pronoms personnels sujets

- Singulier : *I – you – he/she/it*
- Pluriel : *we – you – they*

Les pronoms personnels compléments

- Singulier : *me – you – him/her/it*
- Pluriel : *us – you – them*

Parler de soi et de son quotidien

Le vocabulaire du quotidien

La famille

- mother/father
- grandmother/grandfather
- sister/brother
- aunt/uncle

La maison

- **Downstairs**: kitchen/dining room/living room
- **Upstairs**: bedroom/bathroom

Parler de mes activités

Les activités

- Wake up
- Go to sleep
- Have breakfast/lunch/dinner
- Take a shower
- Brush your teeth

Can/Can't

- **Autorisation/Interdiction**
You can watch TV during the day./You can't watch TV at night.
- **Capacité/Incapacité**
I can swim./I can't play the piano.

Must/Mustn't

- **Obligation**
You must brush your teeth.
- **Interdiction**
You mustn't watch TV at night.

Parler du monde qui m'entoure

L'adjectif en anglais

- Invariable
- Devant le nom

La description physique

- brown/blond/black hair
- brown/green/blue eyes

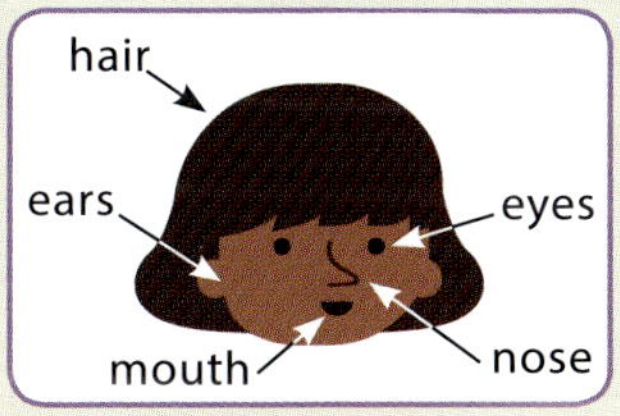

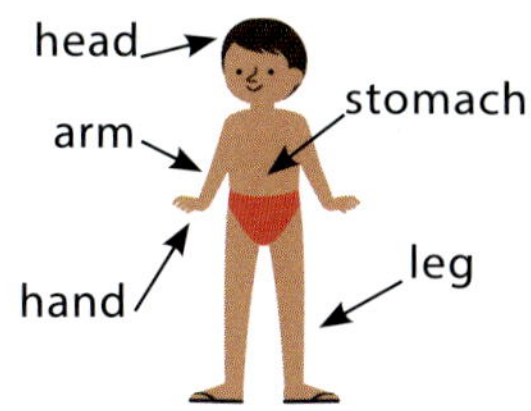

Les articles en anglais

a/an

- **Indéfini :** *a tree*

- *A* + consonne (*a tree*)
- *An* + voyelle (*an apple*)

the

- **Défini, particulier :** *the apple tree*

- *The* prononcé [ðə] + consonne (*the tree*)
- *The* prononcé [ði:] + voyelle (*the apple*)

l'article zéro

- **Indéfini pluriel :** *trees*

There is/There are (il y a)

- **Singulier :** *There is one table.*
- **Pluriel :** *There are two tables.*

Parler du passé

Construction des phrases au prétérit

Forme affirmative

Sujet + BV-*ed* (ou verbe irrégulier)

- *I played video games yesterday.*
- *She ate breakfast this morning.*

Forme négative

Sujet + *did* + *not* + BV

- *I didn't play video games yesterday.*
- *She didn't eat breakfast this morning.*

Forme interrogative

Did + sujet + BV

- *Did you play video games yesterday?*
- *Did she eat breakfast this morning?*

Be au passé

- I/he/she/it **was**
- you/we/they **were**
- pas besoin de l'auxiliaire *did*

Raconter des souvenirs

Voyages

- by train – by car – by plane – by bus – by boat – on foot

- England – Scotland - Wales – Northern Ireland – The United States – Australia – India – South Africa – Canada

- forest – beach – mountains – desert – city
- hotel – restaurant – theatre – cinema – bookstore

Fêtes

- Christmas: Santa Claus – Christmas tree – presents
- Birthday: cake – candles – party

Sentiments

- happy – joyful – glad – excited

- sad – scared – tired – worried

19 *Must/mustn't* p. 32

1 1. mustn't – 2. mustn't – 3. must – 4. mustn't – 5. must.

2 1. d. – 2. a. – 3. e. – 4. c. – 5. b.

3 *Corrigé suggéré :* 1. I must arrive on time/I must learn my lessons/I must answer my teacher's questions. – 2. I mustn't be late/I mustn't talk to my friends in class/I mustn't draw on the tables.

4 1. obligation – 2. possibilité – 3. interdiction – 4. interdiction.

20 Questions et réponses p. 33

1 1. f. – 2. d. – 3. h. – 4. c. – 5. a. – 6. e. – 7. b. – 8. g.

2 1. Where – 2. Why – 3. Who – 4. How old – 5. How – 6. When – 7. At what time.

3 1. When do you have holidays? – 2. Where do you often go? – 3. What do you like doing there? – 4. Who comes with you? – 5. How many pairs of ski boots does she bring?

21 L'impératif p. 34

1 1. Clean the windows! – 2. Bring me my book! – 3. Don't walk on the carpet! – 4. Don't make a noise! – 5. Be quiet!

2 6. – 5. – 3. – 4. – 1. – 2.

3 *Corrigé suggéré :* Go out of the kitchen – In the corridor turn right – When you get to the flower pot turn right again – Go straight on – At the window turn left – When you arrive at the bookcase turn left again – Go straight on!

22 *Be going to* p. 35

1 **Présent :** 1. – 4. – 8. – 9. – **Avenir :** 2. – 3. – 5. – 6. – 7.

2 *Corrigé suggéré :* 1. My father is going to sail. – 2. My mother is going to swim. – 3. My sister is going to eat ice-creams. 4. My grandfather is going to fish. – 5. My grandmother is going to get tanned. – 6. My cousin Elliott is going to windsurf.

3 1. My friends are going to visit London. – 2. We are going to have steaks for dinner. – 3. America is going to send astronauts to the moon.

23 *Whose?*/La possession p. 36

1 1. These are my parents' skis. – 2. This is Tom's ball. – 3. This is Bob's boat. – 4. This is Jennifer's book. – 5. This is John's windsurf board.

2 1. Whose glasses are these? – 2. Whose bag is it/this? – 3. Whose pyjamas are these?

24 Adjectifs et pronoms possessifs p. 37

1 1. my – 2. your, mine – 3. our – 4. our, our, theirs – 5. your – 6. my, ours – 7. your, his – 8. mine hers.

2 1. b. – 2. c. – 3. a. – 4. b. – 5. c. – 6. a.

3 When I opened **my** eyes, I saw Alison's cat. Yes, **her** cat. I hate her. She puts **her** paws on my paper. I often tell Alison: "Take her away! She isn't **mine**, she is **yours**". In fact it isn't **her** cat, it's **our** neighbours'; it's **theirs**. But **my** father's dog ("**my**" dog as he says) often goes into **our** neighbours' house. And they are angry at **my** mother! Because they think she is **hers**. What a mess!

25 Les pronoms personnels p. 38

1 When **I** go and see my grandparents with my sister Sarah, I ask **them** to tell **us** a story. **They** are glad to tell stories to their grandchildren. They have a big book, and when **they** open **it**, **we** are always very excited. Grandfather says: "First I'll read a story for **him**, for Bob. The other one will be for **her**, for Sarah…" And my grandmother says: "What about **me**?"

2 1. them, her – 2. it, him – 3. it, it – 4. you – 5. it, us.

3 1. They like having it at 5 p.m. – 2. He likes eating them with it. – 3. She doesn't take any sugar in it. – 4. They say to us: "Next time bring it with you."

26 Le nom : genre et nombre p. 39

1 1. baby – 2. Mr – 3. woman – 4. son.

2 1. an actress – 2. a brush – 3. a cherry – 4. a church – 5. a dish – 6. a dress – 7. a football match – 8. a tomato – 9. a wife – 10. a witch.

3 1. Postmen bring letters. – 2. Girls like wearing watches. – 3. Young children like listening to fantastic stories.

27 Les démonstratifs p. 40

1 1. this, that – 2. that – 3. this – 4. those.

2 1. this, that – 2. these, those – 3. those.

28 L'article indéfini p. 41

1 1. an – 2. Ø – 3. an – 4. an – 5. Ø – 6. a – 7. a – 8. Ø – 9. a – 10. Ø.

2 1. an American – 2. an hour – 3. a coat – 4. an ice-cream – 5. a uniform – 6. an address – 7. an elephant – 8. a house.

3 1. an – 2. Ø – 3. a – 4. a – 5. an – 6. a – 7. an – 8. a – 9. a – 10. a, Ø – 11. an – 12. a, Ø. – 13. a.

29 *Some, any, no* p. 42

1 1. I'd like some flowers. – 2. Do you want some tulips? – 3. No, I want some roses. – 4. Sorry, there aren't any roses left. – 5. Have you got any chrysanthemums? – 6. I've got some beautiful ones.

2 I thought there was **somebody** at home. I shouted: "Is there **anybody** here?" But **nobody** answered. I was very surprised. I was hungry. I wanted to eat **something**. I went to the fridge. Was there **anything** in it? No, there wasn't **anything** left. **Nobody** at home! **Nothing** in the fridge! Too bad!

3 1. b. – 2. c. – 3. a. – 4. b. – 5. c.

30 Les quantificateurs p. 43

1 1. e. – 2. a. – 3. b. – 4. f. – 5. c. – 6. d.

2 1. b. – 2. a. – 3. c. – 4. a.

3 1. I've got a lot of friends. – 2. There isn't much sun today. – 3. Do you read many books? – 4. Is there much money in your money-box?

31 L'article défini : cas général p. 44

1 1. a – 2. the, a – 3. the, an, Ø – 4. Ø – 5. Ø, Ø, a.

2 1. The students of my class are very nice. – 2. I like watching stars at night. – 3. The mummy I saw was very old. – 4. I do my homework in the lounge. – 5. Soda is my favourite drink.

3 1. I don't like carrots. – 2. I like the houses of my street. – 3. I drink soda. – 4. The songs I prefer are English. – 5. I eat vegetables.

32 L'article défini : cas particuliers p. 45

1 1. breakfast – 2. baseball – 3. the States – 4. bus – 5. Christmas day, last Monday – 6. church – 7. chocolate – 8. the moon, the sky.

2 1. Ø, Ø – 2. Ø, the – 3. Ø, Ø – 4. Ø, Ø – 5. Ø, the – 6. Ø, Ø, Ø – 7. Ø, Ø.

3 1. People go to the States by plane. – 2. The sun is hot in summer. – 3. Dinner is ready. There is fish today. – 4. At school, we play football.

33 L'adjectif — p. 46

1 1. My father's car is black. – 2. This green dictionary is mine. – 3. Some English students wear dark blue uniforms. – 4. Susan has got long red hair. – 5. Bob drives a beautiful green car.

2 *Corrigé suggéré :* tall – fair – long – warm – black – white.

3 1. This is a very exciting film. – 2. The trees in my garden are beautiful. – 3. There are some wild and dangerous animals in a zoo. – 4. Nelson is at the top of a high round column.

34 Modifications orthographiques — p. 47

1 **Pluriel en *-es* :** actresses, addresses, beaches, classes, dresses, matches.
Pluriel en *-ies* : bodies, countries, dictionaries, libraries, stories, universities.

2 1. brushes – 2. dirtier – 3. days – 4. likes – 5. mouths – 6. running – 7. skies – 8. waited – 9. catches – 10. lies.

3 1. buys, brings. – 2. washes, watches. – 3. lazier. – 4. swimming, running.

35 La comparaison — p. 48

1 1. as long as – 2. hotter than – 3. more dangerous than – 4. busier [...] than – 5. more tiring than.

2 1. A Rolls-Royce is more expensive than a bike. A bike is cheaper than a Rolls-Royce.
2. Mary is taller than Jane. Jane is smaller than Mary.
3. a. A comic strip is easier to read than a book. b. A book is more difficult to read than a comic strip.

3 1. Summer holidays are more popular/less expensive than winter holidays.
2. Mathematics is more interesting/more boring than English.
3. Autumn is a wetter/more pleasant season than summer.
4. Playing football is more dangerous/more difficult than rugby.

36 L'adverbe — p. 49

1 1. I always go to school by bus. – 2. I can't always do my homework. – 3. I'm never late at school. – 4. Bob likes school; Alice likes school too. – 5. She likes English very much.

2 1. He never works at weekends. – 2. They sometimes go to the mountains. – 3. We always drink tea. – 4. She feels very well. – 5. I usually go to the theatre.

3 1. Yesterday, Max went to the castle. – 2. He likes visiting old castles very much. – 3. He is never afraid of ghosts. – 4. But he sometimes runs away. – 5. Today, the dragon was very impressive and too aggressive for him.

37 *When* et les prépositions de temps — p. 50

1 1. c. – 2. a. – 3. b. – 4. a.

2 1. at a quarter past seven – 2. in January – 3. from 8 to 11.30 – 4. on Sundays.

3 1. I do my homework until 7 p.m., just before dinner.
2. After dinner, I watch television.
3. I can watch it from 8 to 10 when I am on holidays.
4. I watch it on Saturday mornings too.

38 *Where* et les prépositions de lieu — p. 51

1 1. on – 2. between – 3. near – 4. under – 5. in front of – 6. behind.

2 *Corrigé suggéré :* The window is behind the table. The table is in front of the window, between the door and the window. There is a chair in front of the table and another chair behind the table. On the left, there is a TV-set on a table. There are flowers in a vase on a small table, near the TV-set.

39 La complémentation du verbe (1) — p. 52

1 1. My father often reads German books. – 2. He reads them with a dictionary. – 3. He takes off his shoes. – 4. He takes them off in the corridor.

2 1. e. – 2. a. – 3. d. – 4. b. – 5. c.

3 1. I saw him yesterday. – 2. He took off his hat and he said "good morning" to me. – 3. He looked happy. – 4. He asked me: "Do you want to have a drink with me?"

40 La complémentation du verbe (2) — p. 53

1 **Transitifs :** buy, show, sell
Intransitifs : rise, lie, laugh
Prépositionnels : wait for, look at, think of
À particules : put on, get on, switch on.

2 1. He showed them to her. – 2. He told them to them. – 3. He brought them to her. – 4. The butcher sold it to her.

3 1. up, to – 2. on, for, at – 3. at, at, of – 4. back, down, on.

41 La coordination/Les mots de liaison — p. 54

1 1. so – 2. but – 3. or – 4. and – 5. or – 6. so.

2 1. First – 2. Then – 3. So.

3 **Ordre des images :** 2., 1., 4., 3.
Corrigé suggéré : Batwoman saw a house on fire. First she put on her dress. Then she flew to the house. Finally she saved seven people.

42 La subordination — p. 55

1 1. I'd like to go on holiday. – 2. I like cycling. – 3. I want to spend my holidays in the mountains. – 4. My parents think it is dangerous. – 5. My sister loves reading.

2 1. forgets – 2. thinks – 3. loves – 4. prefers – 5. I'd like.

3 1. d. – 2. a. – 3. f. – 4. b. – 5. c. – 6. e.

18 *Can/can't*

→ Corrigés p. II

J'observe et je retiens

■ ***Can*** **est un verbe modal.**

- Il est invariable.
- Il est **toujours** suivi d'une base verbale.
- Négation → ***can't***
- Question → ***can*** + sujet + base verbale + ?

■ **Emploi**

Can sert à exprimer :

– une **capacité intellectuelle** (phrases 1 et 2) ;
– une **capacité physique** (phrases 3 et 4) ;
– une **demande d'autorisation** (phrase 5).

Je m'entraîne

1 ★★ Mets chacune de ces phrases d'abord à la forme négative, puis à la forme interrogative.

1. The doctor can come before twelve.

a. ....

b. ....

2. My friend Bob can play the synthetizer.

a. ....

b. ....

3. My brother can go to school alone.

a. ....

b. ....

4. Emma can drink milk.

a. ....

b. ....

2 ★★ Comment dirais-tu que…

1. … tu sais nager.

....

2. … tu ne peux pas faire deux kilomètres à la nage (faire à la nage = *swim*).

....

3. … tu n'as pas le droit de conduire une voiture.

....

4. … tu ne peux pas manger de bonbons.

....

5. … tu sais lire l'anglais.

....

6. … tu ne sais pas dessiner.

....

3 ★★★ Imagine que tu as un petit frère ou une petite sœur de 3 ans. En utilisant *can/can't*, écris…

1. … deux choses qu'il/qu'elle sait faire :

....

....

2. … deux choses qu'on lui permet de faire :

....

....

3. … deux choses qu'il/qu'elle ne peut pas faire :

....

....

Auto évaluation Très bien ☐ Bien ☐ Pas assez bien ☐

GRAMMAIRE

GRAMMAIRE

19 Must/mustn't

→ Corrigés p. III

J'observe et je retiens

(1) Bob – It's late. I must go.
Tom – Must you really go?
Bob – Yes, I always go to bed early.

■ ***Must*** est un verbe **modal**, donc invariable et toujours suivi d'une base verbale.

- Négation → *mustn't*
- Question → *must* + sujet + base verbale + ?

(2) The teacher always says we must work hard.
The headmaster says we mustn't smoke.

■ ***Must*** exprime une **obligation**
– qu'on se donne à soi-même (exemple 1) ;
– qui vous est imposée (exemple 2).

■ ***Mustn't*** exprime une **interdiction**.

Je m'entraîne

1 ★ Complète les phrases suivantes avec *must* ou *mustn't* suivant le sens.

1. In the country I .... light a fire.
2. In town I .... cross when the traffic lights are green.
3. At home I .... go to bed at ten.
4. At the seaside I .... stay in the sun too long.
5. At the swimming-pool I .... wear a bathing cap.

2 ★★ Relie les phrases des deux colonnes. Attention au sens !

1. Tom is too young. •	• a. He must drink milk.
2. Harry is a baby. •	• b. He mustn't go out.
3. Mr Smith is an interpreter. •	• c. He must take a taxi.
4. Mr Brown is late. •	• d. He can't drive a car.
5. Peter is ill. •	• e. He can speak English.

3 ★★★ Écris ce que tu dois faire et ne pas faire au collège.

1. Must (3 propositions) ....
....
....
....
....
....

2. Mustn't (3 propositions) ....
....
....
....
....
....

4 ★★★ Quel est le sens des modaux dans les phrases suivantes ? Mets des croix dans le tableau.

	Obligation	Interdiction	Possibilité	Permission
1. What must you do at school?				
2. Can you come to the station with me?				
3. Mother said: "You can't go out. Go to bed!"				
4. You mustn't swim here.				

Auto évaluation Très bien ☐ Bien ☐ Pas assez bien ☐

20 Questions et réponses

→ Corrigés p. III

J'observe et je retiens

MR SMITH – Do you take the 7.30 train?
MR BROWN – Yes, I do.
MR SMITH – Is it a fast train?
MR BROWN – No, it isn't.

MR SMITH – How much is the ticket?
MR BROWN – It's 20 £.
MR SMITH – When do you arrive?
MR BROWN – I arrive at 10 in the morning.

Attention
Who (sujet) + verbe conjugué.

■ Les deux premières questions sont des **questions fermées** ; on y répond par oui ou par non.

■ Les deux questions suivantes sont des **questions ouvertes** : on y répond en donnant une précision.

■ **Construction**
– Si la question est fermée :
Aux./modal + **sujet** + **base verbale**
– Si la question est ouverte :
Mot interr. + **aux./modal** + **sujet** + **base verbale**

Exemple *Who met you at the station?*
(Qui est venu te chercher à la gare ?)

Mots interrogatifs	
who (qui)	**what** (que, quel/le[s])
when (quand)	**where** (où)
why (pourquoi)	**how** (comment)
how much/many (combien)	**whose** (à qui)

Je m'entraîne

1 ★ Relie chaque question à la réponse correspondante.

1. Did you take your case? •
2. Can you carry it? •
3. What did you put in it? •
4. How many T-shirts did you take? •
5. Have you got your ticket? •
6. Where did you put it? •
7. Do you want something to drink? •
8. Who's going to meet you there? •

• a. Yes, I have.
• b. Yes, I do.
• c. Three.
• d. Yes, I can.
• e. In my pocket.
• f. Yes, I did.
• g. My friend Peter.
• h. A lot of things.

2 ★★ Écris le mot interrogatif qui entraîne les réponses suivantes. La question porte sur le mot souligné.

1. Mary is going to London. ....
2. Because she likes this town. ....
3. Peter is coming with her. ....
4. Peter is sixteen. ....
5. They are going there by train. ....
6. They are leaving on Monday. ....
7. At 6 p.m. ....

3 ★★★ Écris en entier, sur une feuille à part, les questions correspondant aux réponses suivantes. La question porte sur le mot souligné.

1. In February we have holidays.
2. We often go to the mountains.
3. I like skiing there.
4. My sister comes with me.
5. She brings three pairs of ski boots.

Auto évaluation Très bien ☐ Bien ☐ Pas assez bien ☐

21 L'impératif

→ Corrigés p. III

GRAMMAIRE

J'observe et je retiens

Max is a robot.
– Max, **walk**.
– **Don't move** your head.
– **Stop** immediately.
– **Shake** hands with me.

Emploi

L'impératif sert à donner un ordre.

- Ordre positif : base verbale.
- Ordre négatif : *don't* + base verbale.

Je m'entraîne

1 ★★ Transforme les phrases suivantes en ordres. Tu t'adresses au robot Max.

1. You must clean the windows.

....

2. You must bring me my book.

....

3. You mustn't walk on the carpet.

....

4. You mustn't make a noise.

....

5. You must be quiet.

....

2 ★★ Tu es dans ta chambre ; le robot est dans le couloir. Tu lui commandes de faire les choses suivantes.

1. Open my English book.
2. Learn my lesson for me.
3. Come in.
4. Walk to the table.
5. Open the door.
6. Go to the door.

Dans quel ordre doit-il les faire ? Inscris les réponses dans la grille à l'aide des numéros qui précèdent chaque phrase.

1er ordre		4e ordre	
2e ordre		5e ordre	
3e ordre		6e ordre	

3 ★★★ Donne tous les ordres nécessaires au robot pour qu'il aille de la cuisine à la salle de bains.

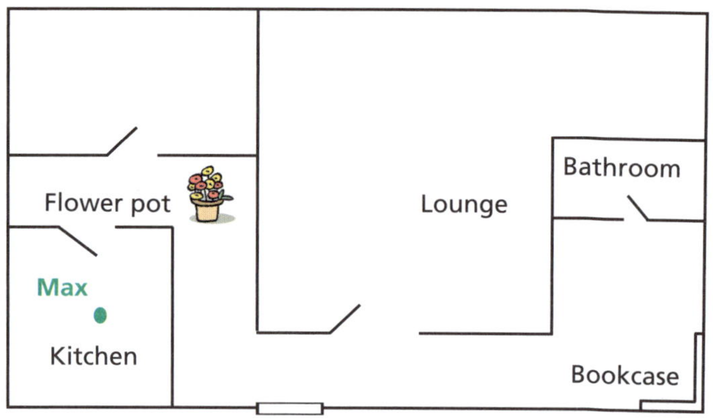

....

....

....

....

....

....

....

....

....

....

....

....

....

....

....

Auto évaluation   Très bien ☐   Bien ☐   Pas assez bien ☐

22 Be going to

→ Corrigés p. III

J'observe et je retiens

The sky is clear; it's **going to** be sunny tomorrow. (1)

Holidays are getting near; we'**re going to** have fun. (2)

What **are** you **going to** do? (3)

I'**m going to** watch television. (4)

■ L'expression ***be going to*** + base verbale :
– renvoie à un **futur proche** ou **lointain** (phrases 1 et 2) ;
– sert à exprimer l'**intention** (phrases 3 et 4).

Attention

Le verbe ***go*** au sens plein (aller à pied, en voiture…) peut se mettre à la forme en *-ing* et est dans ce cas un présent simple (voir fiche 6).

Je m'entraîne

1 ★★ Coche l'une des deux cases selon que la phrase évoque le présent ou l'avenir.

	Présent	Avenir
1. Look! They are going to school.	☐	☐
2. My friend is going to America next year.	☐	☐
3. Tonight we're going to watch a baseball match.	☐	☐
4. I don't know where she is going.	☐	☐
5. Mary is going to have a baby.	☐	☐
6. My neighbour is going to invite me to his party.	☐	☐
7. My brother is going to buy a new car.	☐	☐
8. I'm going to the cinema.	☐	☐
9. Harry is going to his music class.	☐	☐

2 ★★ Toute la famille ira en vacances à la mer. Écris ce que chacun a l'intention de faire *(swim; windsurf; sail; get tanned; fish; eat ice-creams…)*

1. My father ....
2. My mother ....
3. My sister (3 years old) ....
4. My grandfather ....
5. My grandmother ....
6. My cousin Elliott (16 years old) ....

3 ★★★ Fais des phrases en utilisant les éléments suivants. Emploie *be going to* dans chacune des phrases.

1. friends / London / My / visit /.

....

2. dinner / for / have / steaks / We /.

....

3. America / astronauts / moon / send / the / to /.

....

Auto évaluation Très bien ☐ Bien ☐ Pas assez bien ☐

23 Whose? / La possession

→ Corrigés p. III

J'observe et je retiens

MARY – Whose bike is this?
LILY – It's Peter's (bike).
MARY – No, it isn't, not the red one.
LILY – So whose is the red one?
MARY – It's the teacher's (bike).

■ Le **génitif** sert à indiquer la **possession**.

■ **Emploi :** Le possesseur doit être un être animé.

Remarque
On peut omettre de répéter la chose possédée si on en a déjà parlé (**ex. :** *It's my parents'*) ainsi que pour les boutiques (**ex. :** *I'm going to the butcher's*).

MARY – Whose house is this?
LILY – It isn't our neighbours' (house).
MARY – So whose is this house with two large windows?
LILY – It's my grandparents'.
MARY – All right then, you're at home.

■ **Formation**
Le **possesseur** vient toujours en **premier**.

- Possesseur (sing.) + *'s* + chose possédée.

Exemple *Peter's bike.*

- Possesseur (pl.) + *'* + chose possédée.

Exemple *Our neighbours' house.*

Je m'entraîne

1 ★★ **Chacun ses goûts ! Voici ceux de tous les personnages.**

My parents like winter sports. Tom likes playing football. Bob is always on the sea. Bob is a good sailor. John likes big waves. Jennifer is always in a library.

My parents

Tom

Bob

Jennifer

John

Ball

Windsurf board

Book

Skis

Boat

Dans les phrases suivantes, les objets ne sont pas attribués à ceux qui en ont besoin. Rétablis la réalité.

1. This is my parents' ball. ....
2. This is Tom's windsurf board. ....
3. This is Bob's book. ....
4. These are Jennifer's skis. ....
5. This is John's boat. ....

2 ★★★ **Pose les questions correspondant aux réponses suivantes.**

1. .... ? These are the butcher's glasses.
2. .... ? It's Mr Smith's bag.
3. .... ? These are my brother's pyjamas.

Auto évaluation Très bien ☐ Bien ☐ Pas assez bien ☐

24 Adjectifs et pronoms possessifs

→ Corrigés p. III

J'observe et je retiens

TOM – It's my book.

ALISON – No it is not your book. It's mine.

MOTHER – Stop it! Look. It's a dictionary. It's your father's, your mother's, your sister's, your brother's, your grandparents'. It's his, mine, hers, his, theirs. It's everybody's.

Adjectifs	my	your	his	her	our	your	their
Pronoms	mine	yours	his	hers	ours	yours	theirs

- Un **adjectif possessif** est **toujours suivi d'un nom**, un **pronom** n'est **jamais** suivi d'un nom.
- Le choix du possessif dépend du possesseur.

Exemple *Bob's got his book, Jane has got hers.*

Je m'entraîne

1 ★★ Dans les phrases suivantes, souligne les adjectifs possessifs et entoure les pronoms possessifs.

1. SARAH – Have you seen my CD-ROM?
2. BOB – Your CD-ROM? It's mine.
3. SARAH – But it's our computer.
4. BOB – Our computer? No, it's our parents'; it's theirs.
5. SARAH – Dad, can we use your computer?
6. FATHER – Of course! It's not my computer; it's ours.
7. FATHER – By the way, Sarah, this is your brother's CD-ROM; it's his.
8. BOB – Sorry, Dad. It isn't mine; it's hers.

2 ★★ Choisis l'adjectif ou le pronom possessif qui convient.

1. This is .... classroom.
☐ a. mine ☐ b. our ☐ c. theirs

2. This is my table; it's ....
☐ a. my ☐ b. yours ☐ c. mine

3. And that's Bob's; it's ....
☐ a. his ☐ b. hers ☐ c. their

4. There is the teacher's desk; it's .... desk.
☐ a. hers ☐ b. his ☐ c. our

5. This ruler is not Sarah's; it isn't ....
☐ a. her ☐ b. mine ☐ c. hers

6. Sarah, here is a ruler. Is it .... ?
☐ a. yours ☐ b. your ☐ c. her

3 ★★★ Complète avec des adjectifs ou des pronoms possessifs.

When I opened .... eyes, I saw Alison's cat. Yes, ... cat. I hate her. She puts .... paws on my paper. I often tell Alison: "Take her away! She isn't ...., she is .... ". In fact it isn't .... cat, it's .... neighbours'; it's .... But .... father's dog (".............. " dog as he says) often goes into .... neighbours' house.

And they are angry at .... mother! Because they think she is .... What a mess!

> **Attention**
> Le mot *cat* est un mot neutre, ou féminin lorsque le chat est considéré comme un animal de compagnie.

Auto évaluation Très bien ☐ Bien ☐ Pas assez bien ☐

25 Les pronoms personnels

→ Corrigés p. III

J'observe et je retiens

Our teacher, Mrs Smith, took **us** to the British Museum.
We asked **her** to see the mummies (= *momies*).
She answered: "We'll see **them** later. Take out your map!
Hurry up! Take **it** and you'll guide **us**.
Oh, Jimmy isn't here. Call **him**".

Pronoms sujets	I	you	he	she	it	we	you	they
Pronoms compléments	me	you	him	her	it	us	you	them

Je m'entraîne

1 ★★ Choisis le pronom, sujet ou complément, qui convient pour compléter ces phrases.

When .... go and see my grandparents with my sister Sarah, I ask .... to tell .... a story. .... are glad to tell stories to their grandchildren. They have a big book, and when .... open ...., ... are always very excited. Grandfather says: "First I'll read a story for ...., for Bob. The other one will be for ...., for Sarah". And my grandmother says: "What about ....?"

2 ★★ Tu donnes des ordres à Max le robot ; il dit qu'il les exécutera... mais il ne connaît pas les pronoms personnels compléments ! À toi de l'aider à les placer.

Exemple *Give this book to my brother.*
*I'll give **it** to **him**.*

1. Give these books to Sarah.

I'll give .... to ....

2. Bring this cup of tea to grandfather.

I'll bring .... to ....

3. Open the door for the cat.

I'll open .... for ....

4. Bring a blanket to us.

I'll bring .... to ....

5. And now, Max, tell us a story.

All right. I'll tell .... a beautiful story.

3 ★★ Récris ces phrases en remplaçant les mots soulignés par des pronoms personnels.

1. <u>My grandparents</u> like having <u>tea</u> at 5 p.m.

....

....

2. Bob likes eating <u>biscuits</u> with <u>his tea</u>.

....

....

3. <u>Sarah</u> doesn't take any sugar in <u>her tea</u>.

....

....

4. <u>My grandparents</u> say to <u>Sarah and me</u>: "Next time bring <u>your Bingo game</u> with you."

....

....

Auto évaluation Très bien ☐ Bien ☐ Pas assez bien ☐

26 Le nom : genre et nombre

→ Corrigés p. III

J'observe et je retiens

– Who's that person?

– That **woman**? It's **Mrs** Smith. **She** is Peter's **mother**. She's an **actress**.

– Bab**ies** eat with spoon**s**.

– Child**ren** eat with forks and kni**ves**.

– Some **people** do not like police**men**.

■ En anglais, il y a **trois genres** : masculin, féminin, neutre.

- Masculin : *he*, *Mr*, *man*, *boy*, etc.
- Féminin : *she*, *Mrs*, *Miss*, *woman*, *girl*, etc.
- Neutre : les choses, les notions, *baby*.

■ **Le pluriel :**

– cas général → nom + *-s*
– nom terminé par *-s*, *-sh*, *-ch* → nom + *-es*
– nom terminé par consonne + *-y* → nom + *-ies*
– nom terminé par *-f* ou *-fe* → nom + *-ves*
– certains noms en *-o* → nom + *-es*

■ **Pluriel irrégulier :** *child* → *children*

Je m'entraîne

1 ★ Souligne le mot qui n'est pas du même genre que les autres.

1. man / baby / postman / butcher / actor.
2. Mr / Jane / Granny / wife / sister.
3. window / time / money / woman / Monday.
4. sun / son / March / chair / moon.

2 ★★ Voici le pluriel de dix noms. Écris-les au singulier en dessous des images correspondantes.

actresses – brushes – cherries – churches – dishes – dresses – football matches – tomatoes – wives – witches.

1. ....

2. ....

3. ....

4. ....

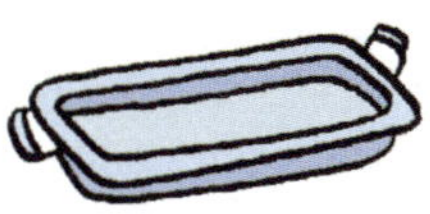

5. ....

6. ....

7. ....

8. ....

9. ....

10. ....

3 ★★ Écris les phrases suivantes au pluriel.

1. A postman brings letters.

....

2. A girl likes wearing a watch.

....

3. A young child likes listening to a fantastic story.

....

Conseil
Aide-toi des phrases en haut de la page.

Auto évaluation Très bien ☐ Bien ☐ Pas assez bien ☐

27 Les démonstratifs

→ Corrigés p. III

J'observe et je retiens

– Do you want **this** cake?
– No, I prefer **that** one.

– What about **these** biscuits?
– No, thank you. Give me **those**.

■ Les démonstratifs sont des **adjectifs** ou des **pronoms**.

Singulier	**this**	**that**
Pluriel	**these**	**those**

■ **Emploi**

– alternative, choix : *This cake or that cake.*
– présentation : *This is Mary.*
– éloignement dans le temps et dans l'espace

Exemple *At that time. In those days...*
He lives in Japan. In that country...

Je m'entraîne

1 ★ Complète avec le démonstratif qui convient.

1. Do you want .... book or .... one?

2. Who's .... girl?

3. What's .... ?

4. In .... days.

2 ★★ Complète les phrases suivantes.

1. .... is my bicycle and .... 's my sister's.

2. .... armchairs are more comfortable than .... chairs.

3. Look at .... stars!

Conseil
That et *those* peuvent aussi exprimer une nuance de rejet ou de mépris. *Ugh! I hate that food!*

Auto évaluation Très bien ☐ Bien ☐ Pas assez bien ☐

28 L'article indéfini

→ Corrigés p. III

J'observe et je retiens

a banana

an orange

peas

a hotel

a uniform

■ ***A*** devant un mot au singulier commençant par **une consonne** (sauf ***h*** non prononcé).

Exemple *a banana.*

■ ***An*** devant un mot au singulier commençant par **une voyelle** (sauf ***u*** lorsqu'il est prononcé [ju:]).

Exemple *an orange.*

■ *A* ou *an* sont obligatoires devant un nom de **métier** : *He's a baker.*

■ **Au pluriel**

- Pour parler des choses en général, on n'emploie pas d'article **"Ø"**.

Exemple *bananas.*

- Pour parler d'une partie de ces choses, on emploie ***some***.

Exemple *some bananas.*

Je m'entraîne

1 ★ Mets *a*, *an* ou *Ø* devant les mots suivants.

1. .... exercise
2. .... parents
3. ...... eye
4. .... umbrella
5. .... chips
6. .... hat
7. .... university
8. .... feet
9. .... hand
10. ..... teeth

2 ★★ Mets au singulier les mots suivants en employant l'article indéfini.

1. Americans ....
2. hours ....
3. coats ....
4. ice-creams ....
5. uniforms ....
6. addresses ....
7. elephants ....
8. houses ....

3 ★★ Complète avec *a*, *an* ou *Ø*.

Tom's birthday list

1. .... electric train.
2. .... videogames.
3. .... horrible witch.
4. .... helicopter.
5. .... anorak.
6. .... tablet.

Exception
Le *h* de *hour* ne se prononce pas.

Betty's birthday list

7. .... interesting DVD.
8. .... nice dress.
9. .... house for her little dog.
10. .... pair of .... tennis shoes.
11. .... English book.
12. .... birthday cake with .... candles!
13. .... smartphone.

Auto évaluation Très bien ☐ Bien ☐ Pas assez bien ☐

GRAMMAIRE

29 Some, any, no

→ Corrigés p. III

J'observe et je retiens

TOM – Is there **any** milk in the fridge?

MUM – I think there is **some**.

TOM – I can't find **any**, Mum.
There isn't **any** milk left.

MUM – Sorry, **no** milk today.

- Positif → ***some***
- Négatif → ***not any***, ***no*** + nom
- Interrogatif → ***any***

Remarques

- Dans une demande polie, on utilise ***some*** au lieu de ***any***.

Exemple : *Would you like some tea?*

- On trouve ***no*** dans les interdictions.

Exemple : *No parking, no smoking.*

- ***Some***, ***any***, ***no*** peuvent se combiner avec ***-thing*** ou ***-body*** : ***something***, ***somebody***, ***anybody***, ***nothing***.

Exemple : *Is there anybody?*
No, there is nobody here.

Je m'entraîne

1 ★ Reconstitue le dialogue suivant (chez la fleuriste) en remettant les mots dans l'ordre.

1. CUSTOMER: flowers / I'd / like / some / .

....

2. FLOWER GIRL: Do / some / tulips / want / you / ?

....

3. CUSTOMER: I / No / roses / some / want / . / ,

....

4. FLOWER GIRL: any / aren't / left / roses / Sorry / there / .

....

5. CUSTOMER: any / chrysanthemums / got / Have / you / ?

....

6. FLOWER GIRL: beautiful / got / I've / ones / some / .

....

2 ★★ Complète les phrases suivantes avec les composés de *some*, *any*, *no*.

I thought there was .... at home. I shouted: "Is there .... here?" But .... answered. I was very surprised. I was hungry. I wanted to eat .... I went to the fridge. Was there .... in it? No, there wasn't .... left. .... at home! .... in the fridge! Too bad!

3 ★★ Choisis la solution qui convient à chaque phrase.

1. The room is empty; there isn't ....

☐ a. nobody ☐ b. anybody ☐ c. nothing

2. There were .... people in the street.

☐ a. any ☐ b. somebody ☐ c. some

3. There are clouds. I can't see .... stars.

☐ a. any ☐ b. some ☐ c. no

4. The door was closed. .... could come in.

☐ a. nothing ☐ b. nobody ☐ c. somebody

5. I want a videogame! Is there .... new?

☐ a. nothing ☐ b. anybody ☐ c. anything

Auto évaluation Très bien ☐ Bien ☐ Pas assez bien ☐

30 Les quantificateurs

→ Corrigés p.III

J'observe et je retiens

(1) – Can I see you today?
– I don't have **much** time, you know.

(2) – Do you sell **many** flowers on Sundays?
– Oh, yes. I sell **a lot**.
– Look! There aren't **many** roses left.

	Dénombrables (que l'on peut compter)	Indénombrables (que l'on ne peut pas compter)
une certaine quantité	***some***	***some***
une petite quantité	***not many*** (négative)	***not much*** (négative)
une grande quantité	***a lot of*** (affirmative) ***many*** (interrogative)	***a lot of*** (affirmative) ***much*** (interrogative)
tout	***all***	***all***

Je m'entraîne

1 ★ Relie les éléments de la première colonne à ceux de la seconde pour former des phrases.

Attention au sens des phrases !

1. There is a lot of… •
2. There are a lot of… •
3. Peter doesn't have… •
4. But I've got… •
5. English people don't eat… •
6. But they drink a lot of… •

• a. sweets on the table.
• b. many videogames.
• c. much bread.
• d. tea.
• e. money on the table.
• f. a lot.

2 ★★ Choisis la réponse qui convient pour chaque phrase.

1. In summer there aren't .... Parisians in Paris. ☐ a. much ☐ b. many ☐ c. any
2. But there are .... tourists. ☐ a. a lot of ☐ b. much ☐ c. many
3. They want to see .... the monuments. ☐ a. much ☐ b. many ☐ c. all
4. But sometimes they don't have .... time. ☐ a. much ☐ b. not any ☐ c. many

3 ★★★ Traduis.

1. J'ai beaucoup d'amis. ....
2. Il n'y a pas beaucoup de soleil aujourd'hui. ....
3. Est-ce que tu lis beaucoup de livres ? ....
4. Y a-t-il beaucoup d'argent dans ta tirelire (*money-box*)? ....

Auto évaluation Très bien ☐ Bien ☐ Pas assez bien ☐

31 L'article défini : cas général

→ Corrigés p. III

J'observe et je retiens

(1) a. I bought **a** record.
b. **The** record was excellent.

(2) a. I like Ø records.
b. These are **the** records I prefer.

(3) a. My cat likes Ø milk.
b. But she doesn't like **the** milk of our milkman.

	Dénombrable	Indénombrable
Nom au singulier	the	Ø
Nom au pluriel	Ø	Ø

■ Dénombrable = que l'on **peut compter**.

■ Indénombrable = que l'on **ne peut pas compter**.

■ **Emploi**

• Si un nom est suivi d'une subordonnée, on emploie ***the*** (phrase 2 b).

• Si un nom est suivi d'un complément de nom, on emploie ***the*** (phrase 3 b).

Remarque

Quand on a déjà parlé de quelque chose, on fait précéder le nom de **the** (phrase 1 b).

Je m'entraîne

1 ★ Complète les phrases suivantes avec *a/an*, *the* ou Ø.

1. Yesterday I bought .... book.
2. .... book I bought tells .... fantastic story.
3. .... story of .... old house with .... terrible ghosts in it.
4. I like .... ghost stories.
5. Poor ghosts! They can't hear .... music, they can't eat .... fish and chips, they can't sleep in .... bed!

2 ★★ Entoure la réponse qui convient pour compléter les phrases.

1. .... of my class are very nice.
a. Students b. The students c. A student

2. I like watching .... at night.
a. stars b. the stars c. any stars

3. .... I saw was very old.
a. The mummy b. A mummy c. The mummies

4. I do my homework in ....
a. a lounge b. the lounge c. lounges

5. .... is my favourite drink.
a. The soda b. Some soda c. Soda

3 ★★★ Traduis les phrases suivantes.

1. Je n'aime pas les carottes. ....
....
2. J'aime les maisons de ta rue. ....
....
3. Je bois du soda. ....
4. Les chansons que je préfère sont anglaises. ....
....
5. Je mange des légumes. ....
....

Auto évaluation Très bien ☐ Bien ☐ Pas assez bien ☐

32 L'article défini : cas particuliers

→ Corrigés p. III

J'observe et je retiens

– They play Ø baseball in **the** States. (1)
– Ø Last Monday, I had Ø chocolate for Ø breakfast. (2)
– I come back from Ø school by Ø bus. (3)
– I go to Ø church on Ø Christmas day. (4)
– In **the** country, I like watching **the** moon in **the** sky. (5)

The
- *the States;*
- *on the right, on the left;*
- *the sun, the moon, the sky, the country, the sea.*

Ø
- repas, sports, pays, villes, jours, mois, saisons ;
- nourriture et boissons en général ;
- *go to school, church, hospital;*
- *turn right, turn left;*
- *go by bus, car, train, plane, boat;*
- *last week, next year.*

Je m'entraîne

1 ★★ Relis les phrases de la rubrique « J'observe et je retiens » puis trouve dans ces phrases les noms correspondant aux catégories suivantes.

1. Repas : ....
2. Sport : ....
3. Pays : ....
4. Moyen de transport : ....
5. Expression de la date : ....
6. Expression avec *go* : ....
7. Boisson : ....
8. Chose unique : ....

2 ★★ Complète les phrases avec *the* ou *Ø*.

1. We eat .... toast for .... breakfast.

> **Attention**
> *Toast* est invariable.

2. In .... summer, ... sea is very warm.
3. I go to .... England by .... hovercraft.
4. I play .... tennis on .... Sundays.
5. .... last week, I went to .... cinema.
6. In Britain, ... children don't go to .... school on .... Saturdays.
7. At .... breakfast, French people often drink .... coffee.

3 ★★★ Traduis les phrases suivantes.

1. Les gens vont aux États-Unis en avion.
....
....
2. Le soleil est chaud en été.
....
....
3. Le dîner est prêt. Il y a du poisson aujourd'hui.
....
....
4. À l'école, nous jouons au football.
....
....

Auto évaluation Très bien ☐ Bien ☐ Pas assez bien ☐

33 L'adjectif

→ Corrigés p. IV

J'observe et je retiens

(1) I'll tell you an **interesting** story. First sit down in this **comfortable** armchair. Do you want a **hot** drink or a **cold** drink? Well, this morning, I bought a **blue** hat, a **short** skirt, **black** shoes and a **long** dress. **Fantastic**, isn't it?

- Les adjectifs sont **invariables**.

Exemple *black shoes.*

- Tous les adjectifs épithètes se placent **avant** le nom.

Exemple *a fantastic English story.*

(2) – a blue hat, a large blue hat
– a short skirt, a short green skirt
– a long dress, a long yellow dress
– black shoes, lovely black shoes
– a fantastic story, a fantastic English story

- Quand il y a plusieurs adjectifs épithètes, l'adjectif de couleur se place juste devant le nom.

Exemple *lovely black shoes.*

Je m'entraîne

1 ★★ Reconstruis les phrases à partir des mots en désordre.

1. black / car / father / is / My / 's / .

....

2. dictionary / green / is / mine / This / .

....

3. blue / dark / English / Some / students / uniforms / wear / .

....

4. got / hair / has / long / red / Susan / .

....

5. a / beautiful / Bob / car / drives / green / .

....

2 ★★ Complète la description de Tom en utilisant les adjectifs suivants :
black – *fair* – *long* – *tall* – *warm* – *white*.

Tom is a .... boy with .... hair and a .... nose. He's wearing a .... sweater, ... trousers and .... shoes.

3 ★★★ Récris les phrases suivantes en tenant compte des amorces données.

1. This film is very exciting.

This is ....

2. There are beautiful trees in my garden.

The trees ....

....

3. In a zoo, some animals are wild and dangerous.

There are ....

....

4. Nelson's column is high and round.

Nelson is at the top of a ....

....

Auto évaluation Très bien ☐ Bien ☐ Pas assez bien ☐

34 Modifications orthographiques

→ Corrigés p. IV

J'observe et je retiens

It was **sunny** today.
George **stopped** for a moment and looked at the **buses** driving past.
He looked **happier** than ever.

Remarque
Mots terminés par voyelle + *-y*, pas de transformation : *boy* → *boys*, *say* → *says*

Dernière lettre du mot	Modification	Noms	De l'adjectif au comparatif	Verbes au passé
1 voyelle + consonne	redoublement	*sun* → *sunny*	*fat* → *fatter*	*stop* → *stopped*
-e	suppression du "e"		*nice* → *nicer*	*live* → *lived*
-s/*-sh*/*-ch*	addition de "e"	*bus* → *buses*		*watch* → *watched*
consonne/+ *-y*	transformation en "i" ou "ie"	*baby* → *babies*	*happy* → *happier*	*try* → *tried*

Je m'entraîne

1 ★★ Classe les mots suivants au pluriel dans la bonne colonne :

actress – *address* – *beach* – *body* – *class* – *country* – *dictionary* – *dress* – *library* – *match* – *story* – *university*.

Pluriel en *-es*	Pluriel en *-ies*
....	....
....	....
....	....
....	....

2 ★★★ Écris les mots ci-dessous en les modifiant suivant les instructions données si c'est nécessaire.

1. brush —pluriel→ ....
2. dirty —comparatif→ ....
3. day —pluriel→ ....
4. like —3ᵉ p. sg.→ ....
5. mouth —pluriel→ ....
6. run —forme en *-ing*→ ....
7. sky —pluriel→ ....
8. wait —passé→ ....
9. catch —3ᵉ p. sg.→ ....
10. lie —3ᵉ p. sg.→ ....

3 ★★★ Récris ces phrases en modifiant les mots entre parenthèses comme il convient.

1. Every day Tom's mother (buy) bread and (bring) it back home.

....

....

2. She (wash) up. Then she (watch) television.

....

3. Her son, Philip, is (lazy) than her daughter.

....

4. He likes (swim) and (run) in the country.

....

Auto évaluation — Très bien ☐ Bien ☐ Pas assez bien ☐

GRAMMAIRE

35 La comparaison

→ Corrigés p. IV

J'observe et je retiens

I'm as intelligent as Tom…
… but I don't get as good marks as him. (1)

Today, planes are faster and more comfortable than they were in 1950. (2)

- Phrase 1 : **égalité** ou **non-égalité** → (not) *as* + adjectif + *as*
  (not) *as* intelligent *as*

- Phrase 2 : **supériorité**

Adjectifs	Supériorité	Exemples
d'une syllabe	adj. + *-er*	*faster*
de deux syllabes terminés en *-y*	adj. + *-ier*	*happy* → *happier*
deux syllabes et plus	*more* + adj.	*more comfortable*

Remarque
Le deuxième terme de la comparaison est introduit par *than*. Le comparatif de *good* est *better*.

Je m'entraîne

1 ★★ Récris les phrases suivantes avec un comparatif d'égalité ou de supériorité suivant le sens.

1. January is (long) … March.

……………………………………………………………

2. Summer is (hot) … winter.

……………………………………………………………

3. A tiger is (dangerous) … a cat.

……………………………………………………………

4. My father is (busy) … on weekdays … on Sundays.

……………………………………………………………

5. Walking is (tiring) … driving.

……………………………………………………………

2 ★★★ Compare les deux éléments en utilisant les adjectifs donnés.

1. A Rolls-Royce/a bike – expensive/cheap

……………………………………………………………

……………………………………………………………

2. Mary/Jane – tall/small

……………………………………………………………

……………………………………………………………

3. A comic strip/a book – easy/difficult

a. ………………………… to read …………………………

b. ………………………… to read …………………………

3 ★★★ Complète les phrases avec un comparatif de supériorité suivant ton opinion.

1. Summer holidays are …………………………………… winter holidays. (popular/expensive)

2. Mathematics is …………………………………… English. (interesting/boring)

3. Autumn is a …………………………………… season ……… summer. (wet/pleasant)

4. Playing football is …………………………………… rugby. (dangerous/difficult)

Auto évaluation Très bien ☐ Bien ☐ Pas assez bien ☐

36 L'adverbe

→ Corrigés p. IV

J'observe et je retiens

BOB – What is she doing **there**?

ALICE – In fact she **usually** comes to that place.
She is **always** waiting.
She was standing there **yesterday**.
She'll be there **tomorrow**, **too**.
She seems to like that place **very much**.

BOB – Look! The street is empty **now**.
Let's go.

■ Il existe **quatre types** d'adverbes :

- **temps** : *yesterday, tomorrow,...* → en début ou fin de phrase.
- **fréquence** : *always, usually,...* → devant le verbe porteur de sens. **Ex.** : *She usually comes.*
  → après le verbe *be*. **Ex.** : *She is always waiting.*
- **intensité** : *very much, too* → en fin de phrase.
- **lieu** : *there* → en fin de phrase.

■ **Place des adverbes** :

Je m'entraîne

1 ★ Récris les phrases en mettant l'adverbe proposé au bon endroit.

1. I go to school by bus. (always) ....
....
2. I can't do my homework. (always) ....
....
3. I'm late at school. (never) ....
4. Bob likes school; Alice likes school. (too) ....
....
5. She likes English. (very much) ....
....

2 ★★ Remets les mots dans l'ordre.

1. at / He / never / weekends / works / . ...
....
2. go / They / mountains / sometimes / the / to /. ....
....
3. always / drink / We / tea / . ...
....
4. feels / She / very / well / . ...
....
5. go / I / to / usually / theatre / the / . ...
....

3 ★★★ Choisis l'adverbe qui convient suivant le sens de la phrase et place-le au bon endroit : ***never – sometimes – too – very – very much – yesterday.***

1. Max went to the castle.
....
2. He likes visiting old castles.
....
3. He is afraid of ghosts.
....
4. But he runs away.
....
5. Today the dragon was impressive and aggressive for him.
....
....

Auto évaluation Très bien ☐ Bien ☐ Pas assez bien ☐

37 *When* et les prépositions de temps

→ Corrigés p. IV

J'observe et je retiens

INTERVIEWER – What time do you start your work?

BUS-DRIVER – I start **at** 7 a.m. I work **from** 7 **to** 11. Then I have a lunch break **for** one hour. **After** lunch I work **until** 4 o'clock p.m.

INTERVIEWER – What about your free time?

BUS-DRIVER – Well, I never work **on** Sundays and I have my holidays **in** August.

- ***at*** : temps précis (**Ex.** : *at 7 p.m.).*
- ***from … to …*** : d'un temps précis à un autre (**Ex.** : *from 7 to 11).*
- ***in*** : période de temps (**Ex.** : *in August).*
- ***on*** : fréquence / jour précis (**Ex.** : *on Sundays).*
- ***after, before*** : *I work before lunch and stop working at 5.*
- ***until*** : jusqu'à (**Ex.** : *I work until 4).*
- ***for*** : pendant (**Ex.** : *for one hour).*

Je m'entraîne

1 ★ Coche la préposition qui convient au sens de chaque phrase.

1. Every day I start my work .... 6 a.m.

☐ a. until ☐ b. in ☐ c. at

2. .... my coffee break, I go to Mrs Brown's office.

☐ a. After ☐ b. Until ☐ c. From

3. I work there .... 1 o'clock.

☐ a. before ☐ b. until ☐ c. at

4. But I never work .... Saturdays and Sundays.

☐ a. on ☐ b. before ☐ c. until

2 ★★★ Écris ce qui correspond à ces images en utilisant des prépositions de temps (*at* – *in* – *from* – *to* – *on*).

1.

2.

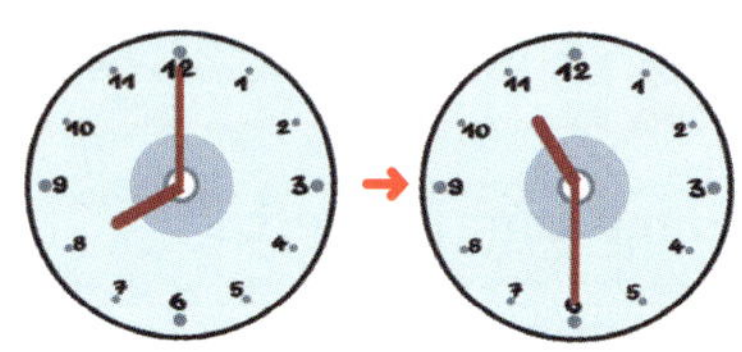

3.

4.

1. ....

2. ....

3. ....

4. ....

3 ★★★ Traduis.

> **Attention**
> Les mots soulignés correspondent à des prépositions.

1. Je fais mes devoirs <u>jusqu'à</u> 7 heures du soir, juste <u>avant</u> le dîner.

....

....

2. <u>Après</u> le dîner, je regarde la télévision.

....

3. Je peux la regarder <u>de</u> 8 heures <u>à</u> 10 heures quand je suis <u>en</u> vacances.

....

4. Je la regarde aussi <u>le</u> samedi matin.

....

Auto évaluation Très bien ☐ Bien ☐ Pas assez bien ☐

38 *Where* et les prépositions de lieu

→ Corrigés p. IV

J'observe et je retiens

 ***on*** : sur

 ***in*** : dans

 ***behind*** : derrière

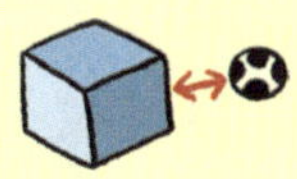 ***near*** : près de

 ***under*** : sous

 ***in front of*** : devant

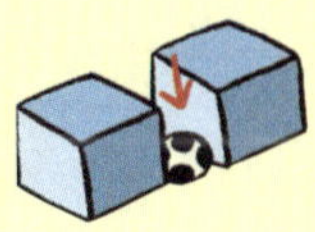 ***between*** : entre

Je m'entraîne

1 ★★ Regarde le dessin et complète les phrases avec des prépositions de lieu.

1. There is a dog .... the back of an elephant.
2. There is a cat .... the two elephants.
3. There is a monkey .... the cat.
4. There is a mouse .... an elephant.
5. There is a zebra .... an elephant.
6. There is a giraffe .... an elephant.

2 ★★ Voici le dessin d'une pièce. Décris-la en utilisant le maximum de prépositions de lieu.

....

....

....

....

....

Auto évaluation Très bien ☐ Bien ☐ Pas assez bien ☐

39 La complémentation du verbe (1)

→ Corrigés p. IV

J'observe et je retiens

JENNIFER – You look tired today.
MR SMITH – Oh, yes. I'm very tired. I'm a taxi driver, you know.
JENNIFER – Take off your coat and sit down.
MR SMITH – No, thank you. I won't take it off. I feel cold.
JENNIFER – All right then. I'll prepare some tea for you.

■ Le verbe *be* est suivi d'un **attribut** qui peut être un **adjectif** (**Ex.** : *I'm tired*) ou un **nom** (**Ex.** : *I'm a taxi driver*).

■ Les verbes *look* et *feel* sont suivis d'un **adjectif**.

Exemple *You look tired.*

■ On appelle verbes **transitifs** les verbes qui admettent un **complément d'objet direct**.

Exemple *I'll prepare some tea.*

■ Pour les verbes à particules, notez la place du COD.

Exemple *Take off* ***your coat****. Take* ***it*** *off.*

Je m'entraîne

1 ★ Remets les mots dans l'ordre.

1. books / father / German / My / often / reads / .

....

....

2. a / dictionary / He / reads / them / with / .

....

3. He / his / off / shoes / takes / .

....

4. corridor / He / in / off / takes / the / them / .

....

....

2 ★★ Relie les éléments des deux colonnes pour former des phrases.

1. Mr Green is a…	•	•	a. very kind.
2. He is generally…	•	•	b. his books.
3. But on Fridays he looks…	•	•	c. relaxed.
4. He forgets to bring…	•	•	d. tired.
5. On Saturdays he feels…	•	•	e. teacher.

3 ★★★ Traduis.

1. Je l'ai vu hier.

....

2. Il a ôté son chapeau et il m'a dit bonjour.

....

3. Il avait l'air heureux.

....

4. Il m'a demandé : « Veux-tu prendre un verre avec moi ? »

....

....

Auto évaluation Très bien ☐ Bien ☐ Pas assez bien ☐

40 La complémentation du verbe (2)

→ Corrigés p. IV

J'observe et je retiens

She **sat down** and **smiled**. She **switched on** the radio and **listened to** music.
Her daughter brought **her a cup of tea**.

- ***Smile*** est un verbe **intransitif**. Il n'a **pas de complément**.
- ***Listened*** est suivi de la préposition ***to***. C'est un verbe **prépositionnel**.
- ***Switched on*** est un **verbe à particule** : *on* change le sens du verbe *switch*.
- ***Brought*** a deux compléments :
  – *her*, une personne ;
  – *a cup of tea*, une chose.

Attention
Veille à l'ordre des mots : personne + chose.

Je m'entraîne

1 ★★ Classe les verbes suivants dans le tableau ci-dessous :

wait for – put on – buy – rise – lie – show – look at – get on – laugh – think of – switch on – sell.

Transitifs	Intransitifs	Prépositionnels	À particule

2 ★★ Récris les phrases suivantes en remplaçant les noms compléments par des pronoms.

Exemple *Uncle Sam gave Mary a present.*
→ *Uncle Sam gave it to her.*

1. He showed his sister his photos of America.
....
....
2. He told his nieces his adventures there.
....
3. He brought Alice souvenirs from America.
....
....
4. The butcher sold Alice a good steak.
....
....

3 ★★★ Complète les phrases suivantes avec des prépositions ou des particules. Choisis-les parmi cette liste : ***at – back – down – for – of – on – to – up.***

Aide
Certaines peuvent être utilisées plusieurs fois.

1. Every day Walter gets .... at 6 o'clock and listens .... the radio.
2. He gets .... the train at 7 a.m. and waits .... a bus .... 8 a.m.
3. .... his office, he looks .... his papers and thinks .... his holidays!
4. When he comes .... home, he sits .... and switches .... the television.

Auto évaluation Très bien ☐ Bien ☐ Pas assez bien ☐

GRAMMAIRE

41 La coordination/Les mots de liaison

→ Corrigés p. IV

J'observe et je retiens

(1) TRAVEL AGENT – Where would you like to go?
CUSTOMER – To an exotic **and** sunny country.
TRAVEL AGENT – Italy **or** Greece?
CUSTOMER – **But** they aren't exotic countries!
TRAVEL AGENT – **So**, Senegal would be all right.

- Addition : *and*
- Choix : *or*
- Restriction : *but*
- Conséquence : *so*

(2) You know I wanted to go on holiday.
So I went to the travel agency.
First the travel agent thought of Italy.
Then he suggested Senegal.
Finally I decided to go there.

- Début : *first*
- Suite : *then*
- Conclusion : *finally*

Je m'entraîne

1 ★★ Complète avec *and*, *or*, *but* ou *so* suivant le sens de la phrase.

1. Mary likes music .... she buys a lot of records.
2. Mary likes classical music .... her brother doesn't.
3. "Would you like tea .... coffee?" the waiter said.
4. At breakfast, lots of French people eat bread .... butter.
5. What do you prefer, apples .... oranges?
6. Peter likes pictures .... he buys comic strips.

2 ★★ Coche le mot qui convient.

1. .... Peter had his breakfast.
☐ a. Then ☐ b. But ☐ c. First

2. .... he had a bath.
☐ a. But ☐ b. Then ☐ c. First

3. .... he felt relaxed.
☐ a. So ☐ b. But ☐ c. Or

3 ★★★ Remets les images de cette histoire dans l'ordre. Puis raconte-la en utilisant les mots proposés et en ajoutant les mots de liaison nécessaires.

1. put on / dress

2. Batwoman / saw / house on fire

3. saved / seven people

4. flew / house

....
....
....
....
....

Auto évaluation Très bien ☐ Bien ☐ Pas assez bien ☐

42 La subordination

→ Corrigés p. IV

J'observe et je retiens

You say you are a good swimmer. (1)
So you like swimming, don't you? (2)
Would you like to swim right now? (3)

■ Il y a trois façons de compléter une proposition par une autre pour faire une phrase :
– les mettre bout à bout **sans utiliser de conjonction** (phrase 1) ;
– utiliser une forme en *-ing* (**base verbale + *-ing***) pour exprimer une généralité (phrase 2) ;
– utiliser ***to* + base verbale** pour exprimer l'intention, la volonté, une demande polie (phrase 3).

Je m'entraîne

1 ★ Comment dirais-tu…

1. … que tu aimerais partir en vacances.
   I'd like ....
2. … que tu aimes faire de la bicyclette.
   I like ....
3. … que tu veux passer tes vacances à la montagne.
   I want ....
   ....
4. … que tes parents pensent que c'est dangereux.
   My parents ....
   ....
5. … que ta sœur aime lire.
   My sister ....

2 ★★ Parmi ces verbes : *I'd like* – *forget* – *love* – *prefer* – *think*, trouve celui qui complète chaque phrase et lui donne un sens.

1. Mr Pemberton always .... to close his door.
2. He .... everybody is honest.
3. He .... taking long walks in the country.
4. He .... walking to cycling.
5. Today he said: "........................ to watch the birds in the forest."

3 ★★★ Relie les éléments des deux colonnes pour former des phrases.

1. The teacher thinks… •	• a. to learn our lessons.
2. He always asks us… •	• b. being interrupted when he speaks.
3. He wants us… •	• c. we'll all get good marks.
4. He hates… •	• d. we are all very good students.
5. He hopes… •	• e. explaining grammar.
6. He loves… •	• f. to do our homework.

Mémo
Tu connais aussi les conjonctions ***because***, ***if***, ***when***.
You must run because you are late.
If you are late, you must run.
When you are late, you must run.

Auto évaluation Très bien ☐ Bien ☐ Pas assez bien ☐

Verbes irréguliers

Base verbale	Prétérit	Sens usuel
be	was/were	être
begin	began	commencer
break	broke	casser
catch	caught	attraper
come	came	venir
do	did	faire
draw	drew	dessiner
drink	drank	boire
drive	drove	conduire
eat	ate	manger
fall	fell	tomber
feel	felt	sentir
find	found	trouver
fly	flew	voler
forget	forgot	oublier
get	got	obtenir
go	went	aller
have	had	avoir
hear	heard	entendre
hurt	hurt	faire mal
keep	kept	garder
know	knew	savoir
leave	left	laisser
make	made	faire
meet	met	rencontrer
put	put	mettre
read	read	lire
ride	rode	aller à vélo, à cheval
ring	rang	sonner
run	ran	courir
say	said	dire
see	saw	voir
sell	sold	vendre
send	sent	envoyer
shake	shook	secouer
sing	sang	chanter
sit	sat	être assis, s'asseoir
sleep	slept	dormir
speak	spoke	parler
spend	spent	dépenser/passer du temps
stand	stood	être debout
swim	swam	nager
take	took	prendre
teach	taught	enseigner
tell	told	dire, raconter
think	thought	penser
understand	understood	comprendre
wake up	woke up	se réveiller
wear	wore	porter
write	wrote	écrire

Lexique

La traduction indiquée correspond au sens des mots rencontrés dans les exercices.

A

a, an: un, une
a lot of: beaucoup de
a.m.: du matin
afraid of (be): avoir peur de
all: tout, toute, tous, toutes
all day long: toute la journée
all right: bien
alone: seul
always: toujours
and: et
angry: en colère
answer: répondre
any: du, de la, des (négatif, interrogatif)
anybody: quelqu'un (négatif, interrogatif)
anything: quelque chose (négatif, interrogatif)
apple: pomme
April: avril
arm: bras
armchair: fauteuil
ask: demander
August: août
autumn: automne
awful: affreux

B

bag: sac, serviette
bath: bain
bathing: de bain
bathroom: salle de bains
bathtub: baignoire
be (v. i.)**:** être
beach: plage
bed: lit
bedroom: chambre
beer: bière
before: avant, devant
begin (v. i.)**:** commencer
best: meilleur
better: meilleur, mieux
between: entre
big: grand
bike: vélo
bird: oiseau
birthday: anniversaire
black: noir
blow (v. i.)**:** souffler
blue: bleu
board: tableau (école), planche
body: corps
book: livre
bookcase: bibliothèque (meuble)
bored: ennuyé
boring: ennuyeux
boss: patron
bottle: bouteille
bowl: bol
boy: garçon
bread: pain
break (n.)**:** pause
break (v. i.)**:** casser
breakfast: petit déjeuner
bring (v. i.)**:** apporter
brother: frère
brush: brosse
busy: occupé
but: mais
butcher: boucher
butter: beurre
buy (v. i.)**:** acheter
by the way: à propos

C

cake: gâteau
call: appeler
camera: appareil photo
candle: bougie
cap: casquette, bonnet
car: voiture
carpet: tapis, moquette
carry: porter, transporter
case: valise
castle: château
cat: chat
catch (v. i.)**:** attraper
chair: chaise
cheap: pas cher
cheese: fromage
cherry: cerise
chicken: poulet
child (pl.: children): enfant
chips: frites
Christmas: Noël
church: église
clean: nettoyer
clear: clair
clever: intelligent
close: fermer
clothes: vêtements
cloud: nuage
coat: veste, manteau
cold: froid
come (v. i.)**:** venir
come in (v. i.)**:** entrer
comics, comic strip: BD
computer: ordinateur
cook: cuisiner, faire cuire
cooker: cuisinière
country: campagne, pays
cross: traverser
cry: pleurer
cup: tasse
cupboard: placard
customer: client
cycle: faire du vélo

D

Dad, Daddy: papa
daughter: fille
day: jour
day-dream: rêvasser
December: décembre
desk: bureau
dirty: sale
disappointed: déçu
dish: plat
dishwasher: lave-vaisselle
do (v. i.)**:** faire (ex. ses courses)
dog: chien
door: porte
downstairs: au rez-de-chaussée, en bas
draw (v. i.)**:** dessiner
dress (n.)**:** robe, uniforme
dress (v.)**:** s'habiller
drink (n.)**:** boisson
drink (v. i.)**:** boire
drive (v. i.)**:** conduire (voiture)

E

ear: oreille
early: tôt
east: est
easy: facile
eat (v. i.)**:** manger
empty: vide
end: fin
ever: jamais (positif)
every + sg.: tous, toutes les + pl.
everything: tout
exciting: passionnant
expensive: cher
explain: expliquer
eye: œil

F

face: visage
fair: blond
fall (v. i.)**:** tomber
famous: célèbre
fast: rapide
fat: gros
father: père
February: février
feel (v. i.)**:** sentir (ressentir)
fight (v. i.)**:** se battre
find (v. i.)**:** trouver
fine: beau (temps)
fire: feu
fish: poisson
fly (v. i.)**:** voler (avion)
floor: plancher
flower: fleur

flower girl: fleuriste
food: nourriture
foot (pl.: feet): pied
for: pendant, depuis
forget (v. i.)**:** oublier
fork: fourchette
free: libre
freezer: congélateur
Friday: vendredi
fridge: réfrigérateur
friend: ami
from: de (provenance)
funny: drôle

G

game: jeu
garden: jardin
gate: barrière, clôture
German: allemand
get (v. i.)**:** obtenir, devenir
get tanned (v. i.)**:** bronzer
get up (v. i.)**:** se lever
ghost: fantôme
girl: fille
glad: content
glass: verre
glasses: lunettes
go (v. i.)**:** aller
go out (v. i.)**:** sortir
good: bon
grandchildren: petits-enfants
grandfather: grand-père
grandmother: grand-mère
grandpa: papy
grandma: mamie
granny: mamie
great: formidable
green: vert

H

hair: cheveux
hand: main
happen: se passer (événement)
happy: heureux
hard: dur
hat: chapeau
hate: détester
have(v. i.)**:** avoir, prendre (un repas, un bain)
have fun (v. i.)**:** s'amuser
he: il
head: tête
headmaster: directeur, proviseur
hear (v. i.)**:** entendre
heavy: lourd
Help!: au secours !
her: son, sa, ses/la, lui (féminin)
here: ici
hers: le sien, la sienne, les siens, les siennes
him: le, lui (masculin)
his: son, sa, ses/le sien, la sienne, les siens, les siennes
holidays: vacances
home: chez soi
homework: devoirs et leçons
hoover: passer l'aspirateur
hope: espérer
hot: très chaud
hour: heure
house: maison
how: comment
how many: combien (pluriel)
how much: combien (singulier)
how old: quel âge
Hurry up!: dépêche-toi !
hurt (v. i.)**:** blesser, faire mal

I

I: je
ice-cream: glace
ill: malade
in front of: devant
inside: à l'intérieur
interpreter: interprète
it: le, la, lui (chose), il, elle

J

jacket: veste
January: janvier
journey: voyage
July: juillet
jump: sauter
June: juin

K

keep (v. i.)**:** garder
kick: donner un coup de pied
kind: gentil
kitchen: cuisine
knife: couteau
know (v. i.)**:** savoir

L

land: atterrir
large: grand, vaste
last: dernier
late (be): être en retard
late: tard
laugh: rire
lazy: paresseux
learn: apprendre
leave (v. i.)**:** partir, quitter
leek: poireau
left (be): rester
left: gauche
leg: jambe
library: bibliothèque
lie (v. i.)**:** être étendu
lift: soulever
light: léger
like: aimer
listen to: écouter
little: petit
live: vivre, habiter
£: livre (argent)
long: longtemps
look: avoir l'air
lounge: salon
love: aimer
lucky: chanceux
lunch: déjeuner

M

make (v. i.)**:** faire
man: homme
many: beaucoup de (pluriel)
map: plan, carte
March: mars
mark: note
marry: épouser
May: mai
me: me, moi
meat: viande
mechanic: mécanicien
meet (v. i.)**:** rencontrer
milk: lait
milkman: laitier
mine: le mien, la mienne, les miens, les miennes
Miss: mademoiselle
Monday: lundi
monkey: singe
month: mois
moon: lune
morning: matin
motorbike: moto
mouse: souris
mouth: bouche
move: bouger
Mr: M. (monsieur)
Mrs: Mme (madame)
much: beaucoup de (indénombrable)
Mum, Mummy: maman
mummy: momie
must: devoir
my: mon, ma, mes

N

name: nom
near: près de
neighbour: voisin
neither: ni l'un, ni l'autre
new: nouveau
next: prochain
nice: joli
night: nuit
no: pas de
noise: bruit
north: nord
nose: nez
nothing: rien
November: novembre
nowadays: de nos jours
number: nombre, numéro

O

October: octobre
often: souvent
old: vieux, âgé
on: sur (lieu), le (temps)
open: ouvrir
or: ou
other: autre
our: notre, nos
ours: le nôtre, la nôtre, les nôtres
outside: à l'extérieur
over (be): (être) fini
overcoat: pardessus

P

p.m.: de l'après-midi
painter: peintre
park: garer
party: réception
paw: patte
pea: petit pois
pen: stylo
people: gens
picture: tableau, image
piece of news: nouvelle
pink: rose
plane: avion
plate: assiette
play: jouer
pleasant: agréable
please: s'il vous plaît
pleased: content
pocket: poche
policeman: agent de police
poor: pauvre
postman: facteur
pretty: mignonne
proud: fier
put (v. i.)**:** poser
put away (v. i.)**:** ranger
put on (v. i.)**:** mettre (vêtement)

Q

quiet: tranquille

R

rain: pluie
read (v. i.)**:** lire
ready: prêt
record: disque
red: rouge
remember: se rappeler
ride (v. i.)**:** aller à vélo
right: juste
ring (v. i.)**:** sonner
roof: toit
room: pièce
ruler: règle
run (v. i.)**:** courir
run away (v. i.)**:** s'enfuir

S

sad: triste
sail: faire du bateau
sailor: marin
same: même
Saturday: samedi
say (v. i.)**:** dire
scared: effrayé
school: école
sea: mer
seaside: bord de mer
see (v. i.)**:** voir
sell (v. i.)**:** vendre
send (v. i.)**:** envoyer
September: septembre
shake (v. i.)**:** secouer, serrer (la main)
shamrock: trèfle
she: elle
shoe: chaussure
shopping: les courses
short: court
shout: crier
silly: stupide
sing (v. i.)**:** chanter
sink: évier
sister: sœur
sit (v. i.)**:** être assis
skirt: jupe
sky: ciel
sleep (v. i.)**:** dormir
slim: mince
small: petit
smell (v. i.)**:** sentir (nez)
smile: sourire
smoke: fumer
so: aussi
sock: chaussette
sofa: canapé
some: du, de la, des (positif)
somebody: quelqu'un (positif)
something: quelque chose (positif)
sometimes: quelquefois
son: fils
sorry: désolé
south: sud
speak (v. i.)**:** parler
spend (v. i.)**:** passer (du temps)
spoon: cuillère
spring: printemps
square: carré
stand (v. i.)**:** se tenir debout
star: étoile
start: commencer, partir
station: gare
stay: rester
stop: arrêter (s'arrêter)
street: rue
strong: fort
student: élève, étudiant
sugar: sucre
summer: été
sun: soleil
sunglasses: lunettes de soleil
Sunday: dimanche
sunny: ensoleillé
sweet: doux, bonbon
sweets: dessert
swim (v. i.)**:** nager
swimmer: nageur
swimming-pool: piscine
switch on: allumer (ex. un poste de télévision)

T

tail: queue
take (v. i.)**:** prendre
take away (v. i.)**:** emmener, emporter
take out (v. i.)**:** sortir (ex. de sa poche)
talk: bavarder
tall: grand
tap: robinet
teach (v. i.)**:** enseigner
teacher: professeur
tell (v. i.)**:** dire, raconter
that: ce (éloignement), cet, cette
the: le, la, les
their: leur, leurs
theirs: le leur, la leur, les leurs
them: les, leur
then: puis, alors
there: là-bas
there is/are: il y a
these: ces (proximité)
they: ils, elles
thing: chose
think (v. i.)**:** penser
thirsty (be): (avoir) soif
this: ce (proximité), cet, cette
thistle: chardon
those: ces (éloignement)
thousand: mille
Thursday: jeudi
tights: collants
time: temps, heure, fois
tired: fatigué
tiring: fatigant
today: aujourd'hui
tomorrow: demain
tonight: ce soir
too: aussi
tooth (pl.: teeth): dent
town: ville
traffic lights: feux tricolores
trainers: chaussures de tennis
tree: arbre
trousers: pantalon
true: vrai
Tuesday: mardi
TV set: téléviseur

U

umbrella: parapluie
understand (v. i.)**:** comprendre
until: jusqu'à
upstairs: au premier étage, en haut
use: utiliser

useful: utile
usually: d'habitude

V

vegetables: légumes
very: très

W

wait: attendre
waiter: serveur
wake up (v. i.)**:** se réveiller
walk (n.)**:** promenade
walk (v.)**:** aller à pied
want: vouloir
warm: chaud
wash: laver, se laver
wash up: faire la vaisselle
washbasin: lavabo
washing machine: machine à laver
watch (n.)**:** montre
watch (v.)**:** regarder (ex. la télévision)
wear (v. i.)**:** porter (un vêtement)
weather: temps (atmosphérique)
Wednesday: mercredi
week: semaine
weekdays: jours ouvrables
well: eh bien !
west: ouest
wet: humide
what: que, quel, quelle, quels, quelles, ce que
what about?: et à propos de ?
when: quand
where: où
white: blanc
who: qui
whose: à qui, dont
why: pourquoi
wife (pl.: wives): femme
wild: sauvage
wind: vent
window: fenêtre
windsurf: faire de la planche à voile
wine: vin
winter: hiver
witch: sorcière
with: avec
woman (pl.: women): femme
word: mot
write (v. i.)**:** écrire
wrong: faux

Y

year: année
yellow: jaune
yesterday: hier
you: vous
young: jeune
your: votre
yours: le vôtre, la vôtre, les vôtres

PEFC 10-31-2065
Certifié PEFC
pefc-france.org

Achevé d'imprimer en décembre 2018 par Pollina en France - 26822
N° éditeur : 2018_0309 - Dépôt légal : Décembre 2018